UNITY LIBRARY 8 ARCHIVES
...iritual education of our
W9-DJE-387

The SPIRITUAL EDUCATION *of* OUR CHILDREN

ALSO BY JESSIE ORTON JONES

SMALL RAIN

SECRETS

A LITTLE CHILD

MANY MANSIONS

THIS IS THE WAY

JESSIE ORTON JONES

The SPIRITUAL EDUCATION *of* OUR CHILDREN

NEW YORK
THE VIKING PRESS

UNITY SCHOOL LIBRARY
Unity Village
Lee's Summit, Missouri 64063

COPYRIGHT © 1960 BY JESSIE ORTON JONES
ALL RIGHTS RESERVED
FIRST PUBLISHED IN 1960 BY THE VIKING PRESS, INC.
625 MADISON AVENUE, NEW YORK 22, N.Y.
PUBLISHED SIMULTANEOUSLY IN CANADA BY THE
MACMILLAN COMPANY OF CANADA LIMITED

LIBRARY OF CONGRESS CATALOG CARD NUMBER: 60-7673
PRINTED IN THE U.S.A. BY THE VAIL-BALLOU PRESS, INC.

BV
1475.2
J718s

But where shall wisdom be found?
And where is the place of understanding? . . .

God understandeth the way thereof,
And he knoweth the place thereof. . . .

Behold, the fear of the Lord, that is wisdom;
And to depart from evil is understanding.

—*The Book of Job,*
XXVIII:12, 23, 28

To

TEACHERS AND PARENTS

CONTENTS

FOREWORD

Education is being called upon at the present time to prepare young people for a future responsibility probably greater than that faced by any former generation in the history of the world. Response to this call is evidenced, in this country, by the enlarged opportunities for study that are being offered in schools and colleges, as well as in the widened scope of the general educational program. However, in this program there is a conspicuous lack in the strengthening of moral training to parallel the cultivation of skills and knowledge. The influence for good in the lives of children which formerly came from homes is also found wanting. Too many parents are simply not measuring up to the demands made upon them by our changing society. All these conditions have become definite handicaps to the full development required of today's youth.

The imparting of moral values involves religion, for morality is rooted in religion. Therefore education is under the necessity of finding an interpretation of religion adequate for today's needs, and congenial to our homes and schools. This can be gleaned from many fields—from history, science, the humanities, the arts, and the ethics of daily living. It should partake of the implicit faith natural to mankind which is reflected in the great religions of the world. Under various names, they all acknowledge One Creator. Each one preaches kindness, temperance, integrity, love of one's neighbor, and reverence for God. When such an inclusive interpretation is found and applied to education, then we may look for a generation equipped not only with knowledge but with wisdom and understanding to meet the well-nigh overwhelming challenges of the world.

The SPIRITUAL EDUCATION *of* OUR CHILDREN

I

TEACHING SPIRITUAL VALUES *in the* SCHOOLS

Let us with caution indulge the supposition that morality can be maintained without religion. . . . Reason and experience forbid us to expect that national morality can prevail in exclusion of religious principle.

—George Washington

As the free world has looked more and more to this country for a convincing interpretation of the freedom it professes, there has been a need, in attempting to meet the challenge, of returning to the ideals of the Founding Fathers for assurance and direction. The re-examination of our national morality has brought into prominence the religious principles on which it rests. The immediate effect of this has been shown in a renewed spiritual awareness along many lines of activity. Churches report a marked increase in membership, and attendance at revival meetings has of late been breaking all records. Newspapers advertise the value of worship in their pages and signboards openly endorse the efficacy of prayer. Secular radio and television programs recommend religion to their listeners. Congress has recently more than once approved a bill that officially confirms this nation's belief in a Supreme Being, and the post office has even been stamping our mail with an exhortation to prayer.

However for one conspicuous reason, at least, the complete sincerity of this religious trend can be questioned. At the same time that greater tribute is being paid religion in daily affairs, it nevertheless continues to be dissociated from education. That which is so ardently sought at the adult level is generally being denied to the young people who must carry the responsibility of a precarious future. The application of the nation's motto, IN GOD WE TRUST, is continually being broadened, yet His name is not often heard in its homes or in its public schools.

There can hardly be any excuse for this fact, yet there are some historical reasons for it. The schools of this country, which were originally established for the purpose of religious instruction, became gradually secularized as differences of opinion arose. The conviction that rigid separation of church and state was necessary for the protection of freedom of conscience became more and more firmly fixed in public opinion. At present, freedom of worship is very rightly being defended in this country as well as freedom of no worship. But there is another freedom which is being overlooked and which should be vouchsafed our children. That is the freedom of an education ministering to their spiritual as well as to their intellectual needs and including them in the upsurge of religious zeal rising in all fields of thought today. We can hardly believe that the Founding Fathers of this country would have desired any less for them.

Many educators are expressing concern lest the secularization of education may have gone too far, for they know that the cultivation of skills and increase of information do not represent the whole of their task. Children unconsciously seek, and should find, spiritual direction, and those who deal practically with them in schools realize this. They know that young people are being deprived of something essential to full development and that school programs are being definitely inhibited. For instance, it is logical to include the study of religious traditions in teaching the ideals of American democracy. Religion enters basically into many other subjects as well. But since "there is no clear-cut understanding of what the schools should or should not do in this field," religion is generally relegated to silence.

An unexpected situation has arisen as a result. "Silence creates the impression in the minds of the young that religion is unimportant and has nothing to contribute to the solution of the perennial and ultimate problems of human life. To be silent about religion may be, in effect, to make the public school an antireligious factor in the community." [1]

It is possible that such an "antireligious" influence in the schools, exerted over several generations, may have had a far-reaching effect on young people. Today there is a failure of homes, as well as schools, to provide moral and spiritual training for their children. The parents in these homes were

[1] American Council of Education, *The Function of the Public Schools in Dealing with Religion.*

the pupils of yesterday and, in their turn, lacked spiritual training. They naturally mistrust that which was not a part of their education. As a result, some young parents seem to fear giving their children any conception of God whatsoever. The opinions of such parents, who are the present-day citizens, are reacting in turn on public schools. They are also creating problems in many church schools as well. Their point of view is making it difficult for certain institutions that exist solely for religious teaching to carry out their purpose. Naturally all parents want their children to grow up to be good men and women, but many do not realize that morality cannot successfully be separated from religion.

I believe that no appreciable improvement can be expected in this condition until there is a quickened awareness, in communities and homes, of the importance of religious teaching, and a willingness to reinterpret that teaching to meet the needs of today. Such a reinterpretation, to be generally accepted, must be approved by people both in and out of sectarian groups. These people would surely represent a fair cross-section of the current religious revival. It would seem logical for them to widen their vision and to extend their zeal to include children. Religion cannot, after all, be considered as relating exclusively to any particular time of life. It might better be interpreted as comprising the whole of life. On such a concept could be based a philosophy of religion comparable with philosophies in other fields and capable of practical application.

Scholastic opinion would, I think, be sympathetic to the idea of such a universal interpretation and could easily find the stuff of religion at the root of every subject now taught in our schools. Literature is a rich storehouse of inspiration and an indispensable vehicle for all expressions of faith and worship. In every branch of science, scientists are coming ever closer, each in his own sphere of thought, to an acceptance of the reality of God. The opinion of Sir James Jeans was that "from the intrinsic evidence of His creation, the Great Architect of the Universe now begins to appear as a pure Mathematician."[2] "Einstein himself [was] strongly convinced of the creation of the universe by a Supreme Intelligence."[3] Anthropologists, in their study of the development of mankind, have concluded that civilizations are born of religion.[4] Psychologists are finding that faith is essential to the mental health of human beings. A new metaphysical dimension, beyond outer form, is being sought in the arts, all of which "may truly be said to have arisen out of religion."[5] Sociologists are teaching social adjustment by recognizing the sanctity of each individual, and comparative historical studies demonstrate the basic oneness of man's faith.

Thus general confirmation gives authority for the integration of a religious orientation with the present curriculum of public schools, and the application of a philosophy of religion to each subject taught there. Examining such a plan would certainly be legitimate. Some experimenting with it would admittedly be necessary. But if there is a chance of

[2] Jeans, *The Mysterious Universe.*
[3] Lincoln Barnett, *The Universe and Dr. Einstein.*
[4] Emile Durkheim, *Elementary Forms of the Religious Life.*
[5] Lewis Browne, *This Believing World.*

finding even a partial answer to what has, for so long, been an unsolved problem, it would be rewarding.

Though avoidance of religion is the usual practice, as I have said, some progress has been made in public schools, here and there, along the line of instruction in objective religion. In some states, recognition and study of the religious heritage of this country is permitted, as well as teaching something about the religious beliefs of the people in the community. In others, the essentials of world religions are taught. Such studies are valuable in clarifying an approach to the new world-consciousness demanded of our country in the present international crisis. It is necessary to see beyond the political fronts of other nations to the traditions and beliefs which have shaped their cultures. Also comprehending the structure and spiritual ideals of our own democracy is of first importance in building the morality of this nation strong enough to withstand the influences that are attempting to undermine it. Those who are courageously giving our children some grasp of these things are making a realistic contribution to the future peace of mankind.

But this contribution, fine as it is, does not fully meet the needs of the individual child. Realizing this, educators have occasionally ventured so far as to "teach the existence of a Supreme Being and to develop an attitude of reverence toward a Supreme Being." [6] These efforts are commendable but still leave much to be desired. Would it not be better to refer to the Deity as "God"? This is an easy and also authentic word which we have inherited from ancient times. It

[6] *The Function of the Public Schools in Dealing with Religion.*

might help a child to feel more comfortable in his attitude of reverence. Religion is an emotional and essentially personal experience. A child's whole character is involved in this experience and his full development waits on it. Repressed, it often leads to inversions of thought and behavior. Released, it proves to be a powerful force for good. In the process of education, therefore, the child should not only gain assurance of the existence of an Infinite Principle in the universe, but he should be led to realize that his own small life is intimately related to a greater, beneficent Life. He must be convinced that he is not isolated, but an important part of the whole orderly creation and that he, himself, lives and moves and has his being in God. This realization is not only deeply comforting to a child but it is a discipline which requires him to recognize equal sacredness in all human beings and so to make his useful contribution to society.

I believe this over-all approach to religion would contribute richly to education. It might eliminate some of the conflicts that are troubling thoughful educators today. It might open up new and more practical ways of presenting the ethics of moral and spiritual values to their pupils. If these things could be brought about, young people might be given better preparation for the exacting tasks which await them.

READING LISTS

The following books are suggested because I have found them to bear helpfully, in one way or another, on the subject under discussion. In subsequent chapters I give lists of young people's books arranged in age groups, though with no idea of arbitrary grading. If the relatedness of some of these titles to religious education is not always easily apparent, it may be because I have rather favored secular books as being more appropriate for nonsectarian use. Their spiritual implications are there to be discovered and interpreted by the individual reader.

All publishers whose locations are not given have offices in New York.

BUTTRICK, GEORGE ARTHUR.

Faith and Education. Abingdon, 1952.

The Preacher to Harvard University here gives four sermons on what he calls "a not-too-easy theme." He believes that education must live within some faith and offers constructive suggestions on how this may be done.

CHAPLIN, DORA P.

Children and Religion. Scribner, 1948.

Here is practical advice to parents and teachers as well as to church schools on various approaches to religion in education.

COMMISSION ON RELIGION AND EDUCATION.

The Place of Religion in Education. Pam. The Church Federation of Greater Chicago, 1958.

A valuable document prepared by The Commission on Religion and Education of The Department of Christian Education, cooperating agency for 1200 churches in four counties. It may be purchased (for 30 cents) from The Church Federation of Greater Chicago, 77 West Washington St., Chicago 2, Illinois.

COMMITTEE ON RELIGION AND EDUCATION.

The Function of the Public Schools in Dealing with Religion. Washington, D.C.: American Council on Education, 1953.

This report on the findings, conclusions, and recommendations of the Committee on Religion and Education presents an exploratory study and substantive data contributed by 3300 educators and 1000 religious leaders from all sections of the United States and from the three major faith groups.

FAHS, SOPHIA L.

Today's Children and Yesterday's Heritage: A Philosophy of Creative Religious Development. Beacon, 1952.

This non-sectarian study describes a philosophy of religion based on the findings of child psychologists and tested by first-hand experience with children.

GRUENBERG, SIDONIE MATSNER, ed.

Our Children Today. Viking, 1952.

The Staff of the Child Study Association of America offers in this book a synthesis of expert opinion on children's needs from infancy to adolescence.

KELLER, JAMES, M. M.

All God's Children, What Your Schools Can Do for Them. Hanover House, 1953.

The Christophers offer this searching study of our subject and a most convincing argument for the need of religion in education.

MARITAIN, JACQUES.

Education at the Crossroads. New Haven: Yale University Press, 1943.

These Terry Lectures on religion in the light of science and philosophy will always be required reading for all who seek a better way at the crossroads of education. They are profound yet simple and very practical. The author reminds us that although the tasks of education are great and mysterious, they may be more humble than many people think.

MEIKLEJOHN, ALEXANDER.

Education between Two Worlds. Harper, 1942.

Tracing the history and background of our present educational system, Dr. Meiklejohn uncovers its weaknesses and sets forth what he believes to be an adequate basis for an educational philosophy in the future.

YEAXLEE, BASIL A.

Religion and the Growing Mind. Greenwich, Connecticut: The Seabury Press, rev. ed. 1952.

The opinion of this authority is that religion is native to all men and is also an affair of the whole person. He reminds parents and teachers of their inescapable responsibility and advises them on the religious instruction of children, both in homes and in schools.

2
RELIGION *and the* STUDY *of* HISTORY

In considering religion, the point to notice is its transcendent importance; and the fact of this importance is abundantly made evident by the appeal to history.
—Alfred North Whitehead

To illustrate the importance of religion in history, we need speak of only one period as an example of the power of faith to carry man to enlightened achievement. This period is within the scope of our continent's history and particularly that of our own country. A flowering from deep religious roots found its fruitage here in the world's greatest democracy. It is a commonplace to say that schools should teach the essentials of our form of government. In this study the religious causes and traditions that went into its inception should be emphasized in order that our children may understand how to preserve their values in the future.

Long before any of the first settlements were permanently established here, it seemed as if this continent had been spiritually dedicated to a high purpose. The cross was always planted beside the flag as explorers claimed the New World for Christ and their crown.

Today the motives and character of Christopher Columbus are seen in a new light. He is now considered not only an explorer and navigator but a crusader. It is believed that it was not so much the need of spices that impelled him to set out for the Indies, as a conviction that it was his destiny to carry the divine Word of the Holy Child across the mighty ocean. "I cannot forget the eternal faith that sent this man forth to the benefit of all future ages," say Samuel Eliot Morison. "The story of Saint Christopher, familiar to every child in the Middle Ages, made Columbus's baptismal name more significant to him than his patronymic. The story would certainly have gone home to the boy Christopher who was father to Columbus the man we know. We may fairly say that the first step toward the discovery of America was taken by the parents of Columbus when they caused him to be baptized Cristoforo (Christ Bearer) in some ancient church of Genoa, one day in the late summer of 1451." [1] This zealous navigator directed religious rituals to be observed on his ship, the *Santa Maria,* which reminded "the seamen every half hour of the day and night that their ship depended for safety not only on her staunchness and their skill but on the grace of God." [1] At every turning of the glass, the young pages said a prayer. With the words of the Psalmist on their lips, they were brought safely, if not to their desired haven, at least to the shore predestined to them.

There are many instances of Roman Catholic dedication in

[1] Morison, *Admiral of the Ocean Sea.*

the history of this country, the settlement of which may be said to have begun in 1565 when Menendez de Aviles landed on the Florida coast and founded a community at what is now Saint Augustine. After the banner of the King of Spain had been raised, a cross was fixed near it and Mass celebrated. From the mission built on this site, padres were sent out to establish the Spanish Mission Trail eventually extending as far as the Mississippi. Later the French explorer Jolliet reached the Mississippi by way of the St. Lawrence River and the Great Lakes. He was accompanied by Father Marquette, the beloved Jesuit missionary who left so many converts along his route. The founding of the California missions was later, when that region was still under the crown of Spain. Located along the Camino Real, the highway which still runs almost the entire length of California, they represent one of the most successful experiments in colonization ever known. However the productivity of their rich lands brought on the envy of later settlers, and many of them were eventually ruthlessly destroyed. But the grace and beauty of their ruins have been left to us, and they are now being authentically restored.

To the east coast of our country came mostly Protestants, who founded the first settlements there on religious principles. Religious persecution had driven Puritans, Quakers, Huguenots, Lutherans, and other sects to that barren shore to seek freedom of conscience. It is impossible to overlook the importance of religion in the life of these early colonies. Many of their political records are actually religious records. The town meetings of New England were conducted much as church services were. The authority of the scriptures was recognized in civil as well as religious affairs. The printing presses were first used for printing religious books. The Puritan schools were founded for the purpose of supplying the churches with a literate clergy and for educating English and Indian youth in knowledge and morality.

The original intention of the settlers toward the natives was generally a desire to convert them to Christianity. If, through a confusion of motives, this zeal later became oppressive, great souls appeared on the scene to champion the cause of justice. Roger Williams established his Providence Plantations as a refuge not only for the Indians but for any others who were, like himself, feeling the sharp edge of discrimination at the hands of the Puritans. In Pennsylvania, William Penn was also living up to his convictions by respecting the rights of Indians and so preserving amity with them. They liked the way this white man called them friends. Elizabeth Janet Gray writes in her biography of this beloved Quaker, "He realized that on his success in establishing friendly relations with the Indians depended the success of his holy experiment, that a government which is good because it is based on religion must begin by dealing fairly and lovingly with the original owners of the land." He always stood by the principle that "the truest means to peace is justice not war."[2]

However, before this peace with justice could be conclusively established in that day, there was a wilderness to conquer and a war to fight. The Revolution was a mighty re-

[2] Gray, *Penn.*

sistance against man's injustice to man, this time with the white man in both roles. But it too was the means of raising up men of great spiritual stature for the need of the hour, and the lives of these Revolutionary heroes surely show the importance of religion in history. Washington at the head of his army or leading the Federal Convention in Philadelphia is no more impressive than Washington on his knees at Valley Forge. Children should be acquainted with this deeply religious man as Father of his Country and also as the reverent schoolboy who wrote in his copy-book, "Labour to keep alive in your breast that little spark of celestial fire—Conscience."

During the dark days of a later war, the spiritual dedication of another great American should be held as an example to schoolchildren. Abraham Lincoln was often found with his generals courageously directing operations on the battle fronts. But he was also often alone, praying Almighty God for guidance. In his second inaugural address he expressed almost a Biblical formula for peace: "With malice toward none; with charity for all; with firmness in the right, as God gives us to see the right, let us strive on to finish the work we are in . . . to do all which may achieve and cherish a just and lasting peace among ourselves, and with all nations."

The just and lasting peace with all nations which Lincoln called for is still the elusive objective of this country. As greater and ever greater moral responsibility is put upon us in this atomic age, is it not imperative that we help our children to a firmness in the right as God gives us to see it? We should be able to direct them toward better ways of achieving peace than ours have proved to be. They, in turn, may sometimes bring fresh vision to their elders.

One day I was showing my child some pictures, in our scrapbook, of the coronation of Queen Elizabeth II. He followed with interest the route of the royal coach through the streets of London. Then, as he looked at the picture of the young queen kneeling before the altar in Westminster Abbey, he asked earnestly, "Isn't this a kind of religion?" I agreed that it was, for the queen was being crowned not only monarch of the state but head of the church. Then we turned to the pictures of the first inauguration of President Eisenhower. There we saw him standing with his hand on the Bible, and I read the prayer he offered on that occasion. "Is our President head of the church too?" was the next very natural question. My reply, that we have no state church in this country, did not seem to satisfy him. He still insisted that this inaugural ceremony also seemed to be religious. I finally acknowledged that democracy is a kind of religion. And then I suddenly realized with what complacency I had made the statement. I believe we all forget at times that the root of our democracy is our faith in God and man in His image. Until this faith becomes a poignant reality to us and our patriotism is translated from a proud boast to a humble prayer, we shall hardly have the spiritual fortitude to withstand the threats that are at present assailing our form of government.

President Eisenhower saw the importance of introducing a religious emphasis into daily life, especially that of our children, when he signed a bill inserting the words "under God" into the pledge of allegiance to the flag. On that occasion, he said: "From this day forward the millions of our school children will daily proclaim in city and town, every village and rural schoolhouse, the dedication of our nation and our people to the Almighty. To anyone who truly loves America, nothing could be more inspiring than to contemplate this rededication of our youth, on each school morning, to our country's true meaning. Especially is this meaningful as we regard today's world. Over the globe, mankind has been cruelly torn by violence and brutality and, by the millions, deadened in the mind and soul by a materialistic philosophy of life. Man everywhere is appalled by the prospect of atomic war. In this way we are reaffirming the transcendence of religious faith in America's heritage and future; in this way we shall constantly strengthen those spiritual weapons which forever will be our country's most powerful resource in peace or in war."

In teaching history, then, let our country's true meaning be stressed. Let the transcendence of religious faith in it be fully explained in public classrooms and presented to the young people who are the heirs of America's heritage. Then will they be provided with the spiritual weapons which are indeed the most powerful resource under any and all circumstances.

READING LISTS

BRADFORD, WILLIAM.

Of Plymouth Plantation, 1620–1647. Knopf, 1952.

The official chronicle written by Plymouth's first governor, the substance of which has entered into American folklore, is here put into modernized text by the Harvard scholar Samuel Eliot Morison.

COUSINS, NORMAN, ed.

In God We Trust. Harper, 1958.

The religious beliefs and ideas of the Founding Fathers who came together to design not only a nation but a way of life.

FRANKLIN, BENJAMIN.

Autobiography. Harper, 1956.

This record of a great man, written by his own hand, gives an intimate account of his printing experience, his inventing, soldiering, writing, and his diplomacy and philosophy, which have come to be the backbone of Americanism.

MORISON, SAMUEL ELIOT.

Admiral of the Ocean Sea: A Life of Christopher Columbus. Little, Brown, 1942.

No one should miss the opportunity of sailing with this experienced mariner and scholarly historian over the routes taken by Columbus. He gives, in this book, a wealth of information and the atmosphere of the original ships' logs.

MOWAT, R. C.

Climax of History. London: Blandford Press, 1951.

As Senior Lecturer in History at the Royal Naval College at Greenwich, the author is well equipped to interpret the present trends in history and to analyze the world's needs. He sees the necessity of meeting the ideology of Communism with an equally strong faith in what we, in America, believe to be a better way of life. And he finds that Moral Re-Armament, under the leadership of Frank Buchman, offers a religious ideology which he considers eminently practical for that purpose.

REPPLIER, AGNES.

Junipero Serra, Pioneer Colonist of California. Doubleday, rev. ed. 1947.

A learned biography of a great man and near-saint to whom we are indebted for a most picturesque chapter in the religious history of America.

SANDBURG, CARL (introd. by).

The Lincoln Devotional. Channel Press, 1957.

A daily spiritual guide used by Abraham Lincoln, beautifully introduced by one of his greatest admirers.

TOYNBEE, ARNOLD.

An Historian's Approach to Religion. Oxford, 1956.

This profound historian names "self-centeredness" as the original sin in his philosophy, and love as the greatest good. Through a true interpretation of democracy, he believes this might be attained.

WINSLOW, OLA ELIZABETH.

Master Roger Williams: A Biography. Macmillan, 1957.

The life of this prophet of "soul-freedom" is here frankly told, with no softening of his weary experiences with the early Colonies and with a fine appreciation of his contribution to religious freedom in this country.

Books for Young People

Elementary

AULAIRE, INGRI and EDGAR D'.

George Washington. Il. by the authors. Doubleday, 1936.

A charmingly illustrated story of the Father of our Country.

DALGLIESH, ALICE.

The Columbus Story. Il. by Leo Politi. Scribner, 1955.

Though written for young children, this book is none the less authoritative. Some of Columbus's actual words and a song sung by his boy sailor are quoted.

DE ANGELI, MARGUERITE.

Thee, Hannah! Il. by the author. Doubleday, 1940.

Quaint traditions of Quaker home life and beliefs in a Philadelphia family before the Civil War.

HAYS, WILMA PITCHFORD.

Pilgrim Thanksgiving. Il. by Leonard Weisgard. Coward-McCann, 1955.

An authentic story of the first Thanksgiving, made particularly attractive to young readers.

LAWSON, ROBERT.

They Were Strong and Good. Il. by the author. Viking, 1940.

It is wholesome for children to know about their good ancestors in this country.

MURPHY, RUBY BRADFORD.

American Riddles in Rhyme. Il. by John Dukes McKee. Abingdon, 1955.

Your child, with this book in his hand, may monopolize the living room with riddles, but he will be learning, and teaching, American history.

POLITI, LEO.

Mission Bell. Il. by the author. Scribner, 1953.

The touching story, beautifully told and pictured, of the ringing of the bell at the first mission in California with the Indians timidly arriving for Mass.

TOOZE, RUTH.

America. Decorated by Valenti Angelo. Viking, 1956.

This rhythmic prose-poetry, delightfully embellished, gives children a profound lesson about America in a most pleasant form.

TUNIS, EDWIN.

Colonial Living. Il. by the author. World, 1957.

A book especially recommended to teachers in the lower grades because of its interesting information on the many details of daily life in the Colonies.

Intermediate

BAUER, HELEN.

California Mission Days. Doubleday, 1951.

Beautiful photographs of the missions as they appear today, and old prints showing them as they were originally constructed give a background to this authentic story of the beloved Fra Serra and his founding of many of these same missions.

FISHER, DOROTHY CANFIELD.

Our Independence and the Constitution. Il. by Robert Doremus. Random, 1950.

This book is a must for every child in this country, whether native or not.

HAVILAND, VIRGINIA.

William Penn, Founder and Friend. Il. by Peter Burchard. Abingdon-Cokesbury, 1952.

A sympathetic story of this great Friend from his childhood to his maturity, when he worked so tirelessly for religious freedom.

JUDSON, CLARA INGRAM.

Benjamin Franklin. Il. by Robert Frankenberg. Chicago: Follett, 1957.

A lively portrait which takes Franklin from his early apprenticeship to a printer in Boston through his important years as diplomat and humanitarian, closing with his last days in Philadelphia.

LE SUEUR, MERIDEL.

The River Road: A Story of Abraham Lincoln. Il. by Aldren A. Watson. Knopf, 1954.

An important book, not only for its information on the life of Abraham Lincoln, but for the experience it gives in sharing the hopes and ideals of a great soul.

MIERS, EARL SCHENCK.

Rainbow Book of American History. Il. by James Daugherty. World, 1955.

No one could read this book without feeling great pride in America and in the idealists who shaped its destiny. It is a lesson in patriotism.

NORTH, STERLING.

George Washington: Frontier Colonel. Il. by Lee Ames. Random, 1957.

In his usual fresh style, the author gives authentic pictures of George's early life, his surveying years, his part in the French and Indian War, and finally of the master of Mount Vernon and Father of his Country.

PETERSHAM, MAUD and MISKA.

Story of the Presidents of the United States of America. Il. by the authors. Macmillan, 1953.

This is an excellent text made more expansive by the illustrations. A brief biography of each President is given, and, at the end, the presidential portrait stamps are shown.

UPDEGRAFF, FLORENCE. M.

Traveler's Candle. Il. by Eva A. Watson. Harcourt, 1942.

An open door and a warm hearth bring Indians confidently to a Quaker home in colonial days, where their Great Spirit is respected even as is the white man's God. Now out of print, this book is worth looking for in libraries and old bookshops.

Advanced

BAINTON, ROLAND H.

The Church of Our Fathers. Scribner, rev. ed. 1941.

Here is an impressive history of the Christian Church—how it came to be in the days of Jesus and how it has continued into the present. In the conclusion, the eventual separation of Church and State in this country is referred to with the statement that this did not mean that religion was to be taken out of teaching.

COURNOS, JOHN.

Pilgrimage to Freedom: Story of Roger Williams. Il. by Rus Andersen. Holt, 1953.

This biography of Roger Williams gives the dramatic tale of his good relations with the Indians as well as the less happy associations with the church people of Boston and Salem.

DAUGHERTY, JAMES.

Poor Richard. Il. by the author. Viking, 1941.

Another splendid biography of Benjamin Franklin, whose name stands with the great ones of our country. The illustrations add much to the text.

EIFERT, VIRGINIA S.

Out of the Wilderness: Young Abe Lincoln Grows Up. Il. by Manning De V. Lee. Dodd, 1956.

An eloquent narrative relating the hard early years of young Abe Lincoln in Kentucky, Indiana, and Illinois.

FOSTER, GENEVIEVE.

George Washington's World. Il. by the author. Scribner, 1941.

The broad sweep of his author's world-view always gives important perspective to any phase of history she chooses for her subject.

GRAY, ELIZABETH JANET.

Penn. Il. by George Whitney. Viking, 1938.

A study of a great Quaker by another Quaker who has made her own unique contribution to international relations.

LISITZKY, GENE.

Thomas Jefferson Il. by Harrie Wood. Viking, 1933.

A most important contribution to the literature of American history. It is accurate, well balanced, and charmingly written.

MORISON, SAMUEL ELIOT.

The Story of the Old Colony of New Plymouth 1620–1692. Il. by Charles H. Overly. Knopf, 1956.

An unexpected touch of humor is reported here as a part of the Pilgrim thought and many sidelights are given which soften our accustomed opinions of life in old Plymouth.

SHIPPEN, KATHERINE B.

The Great Heritage. Il. by C. B. Falls. Viking, 1947.

Valuable maps and illustrations emphasize the important record of our heritage from the land and from the men who have made America.

WISE, WILLIAM.

Silversmith of Old New York: Myer Myers. Il. by Leonard Everett Fisher. Farrar, 1958.

Myer Myers, son of one of the earliest Jewish settlers in the colonies, became a skilled silversmith and a famous patriot. The tale of his many services to the American cause, including that of carrying bullets through enemy lines, is a thrilling one.

3
A SPIRITUAL APPROACH *to* SCIENCE

The dominating principle in the art of teaching all things to all men, should be, and can be, borrowed from no other source but the operations of nature. . . . We seek God by noticing the signs of His divinity in all things created.

—*Comenius*

Particularly challenging at this time is the task of teaching science idealistically. For these studies have become involved with the political world of international competition in destructive weapons. An authority in that field seems to be defining the first requirement when he says: "Today, more than ever before, our survival—yours and mine and our children's—depends on our adherence to ethical principles. Ethics alone will decide whether atomic energy will be an earthly blessing or the source of mankind's utter destruction." [1] Scientists generally recognize a morality intrinsic in nature which places all of life under the discipline of a transcendent

[1] Wernher von Braun in *This Week Magazine,* January 24, 1960.

Law. They, perhaps more than any others, realize the importance of instilling respect for this Law in young people and of instructing them in reverence for its Author.

The Bible opens with a description of God as Maker of heaven and earth. The great Song of Creation in the first chapter of Genesis makes a good introduction to Him for our children. It offers allegorically a preview of science presaging the whole cycle of life. Its evening and morning refrains punctuate the stanzas of nature's unfoldment, and the sequences of its narrative mark the stages of evolution on this earth. "In the beginning, God created"—here is a fundamental truth to start with. It leads swiftly to a conviction that what God created He meant to maintain. For He looked with favor upon His creation at each stage of its growth. From void and darkness, He created light and saw that it was good. As His spirit moved upon the face of the waters, His plan of life evolved and He blessed it.

Children love to trace the divine pattern in this mystical poem. They delight in the description of the safe dry land on which we live, as the waters are drawn from it and gathered conveniently together. Their first lesson in herb, fruit, and seed comes next, even to that great mystery of persistence of species—"the herb yielding seed after its kind, and the tree yielding fruit, whose seed was in itself, after its kind."

As they go on to learn of the creation of the heavenly bodies and to the appearance of the strange forms that swim and fly and crawl, the First Cause of Spirit becomes apparent. It is emphasized over and over again in the simple reiterations: "And God said . . . And God called . . . And God created . . . And God blessed . . . And God saw every thing that He had made, and, behold, it was very good."

The climax of this thrilling story comes at the end, when God created man—"male and female created He them." That means us, and, wonder of wonders, He created us in His own image. And, marvel of marvels, He gave us dominion over all His former creations—herb and tree, fish, fowl, and beast. He gave man all this responsibility. But He also gave him His own likeness of mind and soul with which to fulfill it.

After so inspiring a survey of the whole universe, it may take some effort to concentrate on one or another of its aspects for practical study. Each child should be left free to choose the field of his special interest. Stimulated by today's space exploration, many will want books and lessons which take them into the firmament. Others will become botanists, yet others geologists or anthropologists. Every science schoolroom should be equipped with an adequate bookshelf and with facilities for all manner of experiments to meet these interests. Sunny windows should be filled with sprouting seeds and growing plants to watch. Birds should be invited to feeding shelves outside, and small animals kept as friends within. Ants, which will obligingly carry on their activities in jars of sand, may be studied through the glass walls. Bees will exhibit their hive society in a proper box fitted into some lower sash. An egg or larva of the monarch butterfly on a stalk of milkweed will offer one of the most rewarding of all nature's shows. The monarch completes its life cycle from egg to butterfly in a few weeks, and each stage of its growth is a wonder to behold. Its final metamorphosis is a veritable miracle, for it demonstrates, before our eyes, a cellular change from a crawling creature to a flying one. If it is possible for a school to have a telescope available, this might bring students the most valuable of all lessons. For the law and order of the heavens speak very directly to the problems of earth. A parallel is logical between the fixed pole star, with the constellations wheeling about it, and the varied patterns of human thought continually moving about the Still Center which is God. As children learn how a mariner charts his course by Polaris, so may they be taught that God is the lodestar of their lives.

Today's scientists are continually recognizing such parallels. One of their greatest has called religion and science "twin offspring of man's quest for an understanding of his world." [2] An eminent physicist says, "Scientific faith in the rational order of nature and religious faith in a Divine Mind have a common origin." [3] Jean Henri Fabre saw religious implications in his study of the earth. "If the heavens declare the glory, the power and the majesty of God," he said, "to whom as first cause we ascribe all things, does not also the rent and agitated bosom of our mother earth speak of God's never-ceasing care of his creatures?" [4] As Fabre invited his readers to explore with him earth's inner structure, he promised them, "We shall bring back from our underground journey no precious stones or costly metals, but something better—sublime conceptions of the architecture of this globe

[2] Carnegie Foundation for the Advancement of Teaching, *48th Annual Report.*

[3] Paul E. Sabine, *Atoms, Men, and God.*

[4] Fabre, *This Earth of Ours.*

of ours and a high admiration for its divine Architect." The same scientist, who devoted fifty years of solitary existence to the study of insects, brought a wealth of wisdom from that field. Always his approach was religious, bowing, as he said, "before these mysteries of life to the Author of these miracles." [4] His friend and colleague Maurice Maeterlinck found in the ant and the bee "an immortal collective soul." [5] Both of them subscribed to what Emerson called "the true doctrine of omnipresence—that God reappears with all His parts in every moss and cobweb." [6]

I offer these quotations as a sample of authentic material on which to base the teaching of spiritual values through science. But any attempt on my part to outline a specific method of accomplishing this would seem to me to be presumptuous. For the success of such teaching depends upon the relation between the individual teacher and pupil. And it calls for a certain intuition capable of distilling truth from a bewildering universe and applying it to the sensitive needs of the human heart. "Truth," says Lewis Browne, "is incapable of being organized. It belongs generically to the realm of the ideal and it can no more be regimented than the rainbow can be hung with clothes." [7]

Yet there was a great educator, back in the seventeenth century, who gave his life to working out a system of integrating religion with general education. John Comenius has

[5] Maeterlinck, *The Life of the Bee.*
[6] Ralph Waldo Emerson, essay on "Compensation."
[7] *This Believing World.*

been called "the most penetrating writer on method whom the world has ever seen." [8] "The teaching of a child seemed to him analogous to the cultivating of a plant. The action of education was like that of the sun. And from this it followed that all learning should be patterned after the processes of growth as seen in natural objects. He had two basic presuppositions—the unity of knowledge and the unity of mankind. . . . They are two different sides of his belief in God. . . . If we should ask Comenius why knowledge is one, his religious answer is clear and unequivocal. Knowledge, as we have it, is knowledge by man of the world. And both man and world are created by God, each with reference to the other. . . . When men engage in scientific study, therefore, they are not simply following the drives of their own curiosity and intelligence. They are, by that very act, following after the meaning and intention of the Creator both of themselves and of the objects of their study. . . . If we ask what is the social group whose pattern of culture the teacher must follow, the answer of Comenius is very direct. It is the society of mankind, held together as a single society by a common sonship to God. The brotherhood of man is not for Comenius an idle phrase. It is the fundamental fact upon which all education rests." [9]

In *The Great Didactic,* Comenius recommends that "we seek a method of instruction by which teachers may teach less, and learners may learn more." When both stand hum-

[8] Simon Laurie, *Studies in the History of Educational Opinion from the Renaissance.*

[9] Alexander Meiklejohn, *Education between Two Worlds.*

bly before nature, the great Teacher, and learn together, they may share some priceless lessons, and the sharing of them is the pearl of great price in teaching. One day when a wave had washed up at the feet of my child a stone containing a fossil, our familiar beach became truly a "seashore of endless worlds." [10] The four-year-old who wonderingly traced the spiral with his finger was not too young to enjoy an expedition later on to a museum with our treasure. His books had somewhat prepared him for the curator's verdict that we had found a cephalopod, relic of the Devonian age, and he took the three hundred million years of pre-history in his small stride. I believe his growing conviction that fossils are "the most important of all things" has added a stratum of stability to his character. Impressions in stones depict a great story. They show such molding of form to circumstance and even shaping of circumstance to life's needs, that our faith expands as we study them. No infinitesimal purpose, it seems, is overlooked in the working out of God's plan.

Fossils are important not only as records of animal life but also their delicate imprints of plant life open another world of wonder. The herb of the field which God bestowed upon man in the beginning preaches a silent sermon. "The botanist delights in observing how the tens of thousands of kinds of plants all harmonize with each other, like the parts of concerted music, plainly showing that they were all contrived, as parts of one system, by one Divine Mind." [11] "We are wholly dependent upon this green society," says Donald

[10] Rabindranath Tagore, *Gitanjali.*
[11] Asa Gray, *How Plants Grow.*

Culross Peattie, "this serene sister life; it reaches farther over and into our common earth and leaves a deeper imprint there than we do or our fellow creatures." [12] Let us introduce our children to this serene sister, not only by means of books but, at first hand, in our own gardens. Let us discover there together the perfect faith of plants which, though rooted to the ground, contrive to attract plenty of messengers to run their pollen errands for them and winds to carry their seeds to the ends of the earth. Let us teach our children the parables of the garden, for:

> Earth's crammed with heaven,
> And every common bush afire with God.[13]

The evolution of the strange animal forms that developed as life unfolded on this planet tells what an eminent scientist calls, "the biggest story ever, the tale that out-sagas, out-epics and out-dramas every other saga, epic or drama." [14] That is what children are looking for today—the superlative story that will dwarf all others. They will not be disappointed in the chapters of this great epic containing the first amphibians, the dinosaurs and giant lizards. I think they will also be thrilled to make the acquaintance of their ancestor—Homo sapiens. When Darwin first gave out his theory of the evolution of this man from the lower forms, he really frightened our grandfathers, who feared their religion would be undermined. There was a search being made at that time for the "missing link" that might root our family tree in monkey

[12] *Flowering Earth.*
[13] Elizabeth Barrett Browning, "Aurora Leigh."
[14] Gerald Heard, *Gabriel and the Creatures.*

stock, and an ancestor who went on all fours did not seem to be one created in the image of God. Our children need not be troubled by such fears today. What seemed so terrifying has become a part of greater discoveries. "Darwin was wrong, but right," says Ruth Moore. "Darwin's theory of evolution is being modified. Suddenly research answered some of the unanswered questions about how man evolved and the rate at which he evolved. The new fossils filled in and changed the record of man." [15]

Science now says that all life is still in process, with infinite growing possibilities ahead. The image of God is emerging slowly in man, but it would be logical for Him to take at least as long to evolve a soul as it has taken fish to grow legs or reptiles wings! The encouraging thing is that, from his earliest days, man has been ceaselessly striving for a concept of his Maker that would help him to understand life as he should live it. It is reassuring to know that religion is basic to human thought and not something lately invented to apply to our present dilemma.

Worship finds expression in many idioms, both past and present. Sometimes God has been thought of as divine Mother. This matriarchal influence may account for certain long periods of peace in Neolithic times. The primitive prototype of the European Earth Mother was Mother Corn to the American Indian. She was the personification of the cereal supply which once brought these early people to a high state of development. Her mate was Father the Sky. These

[15] *Man, Time, and Fossils.*

two were the Parents of Creation in the Indian tradition. None of these concepts can be perfect at the human level of revelation and they are usually tainted with superstition. But all indicate a sincere striving to understand the divine impact upon human life.

Archaeology is one way of studying existence remote from our times. Another is by acquaintance with people of today who have made so little progress that they may be taken as examples of life as it was lived thousands of years ago. Such people enable anthropologists to glimpse the characteristics of our far-off ancestors. Myths and rituals, handed down by word of mouth from the past, are their contribution to the present. These indicate that man has always had some capacity for faith in God. Said an old African chieftain, "There are more things above us than all the books of the whites contain." His people acknowledge an invisible Sovereign Master to whom they pray, "Our Father in Heaven." [16] They believe in the immortality of the human soul, which at death passes into another existence.

So it is that the thread of religion runs naturally through all the sciences and binds them together. Without transgressing any law of our land and without indoctrinating a single child, I am sure that we may safely emphasize this supreme unity and teach it. The presence of a great First Cause in the universe is everywhere apparent. Finding nature's God in and through His whole creation confirms the individual and stabilizes his relationship with his fellows. Through such

[16] Alexandre LeRoy, *Religion of the Primitives.*

faith it becomes possible to face the invisible mystery of life and death without fear, for it gives assurance that "God saw every thing that He had made, and, behold, it was very good."

READING LISTS

COMPTON, ARTHUR H.

Atomic Quest; a Personal Narrative. Oxford, 1956.

To this distinguished scientist, God is a beneficent, creative Power acting through all men. He is quoted as saying, at a meeting of the American Physical Society, that the "laws of physics leave room for an immanent God. They have removed what has been a barrier against believing in such a God."

HEARD, GERALD.

Gabriel and the Creatures. Il. by Susanne Suba. Harper, 1952.

This book opens with a group of very small prehistoric lizards holding a meeting which is attended by the Angel Gabriel to grant them two wishes from the utterly wise Divine Will. With the authority of an anthropologist, but with tongue in cheek, the author proceeds to tell the story of evolution in an irresistibly sparkling way.

HUXLEY, JULIAN.

New Bottles for New Wine. Harper, 1958.

One of the world's most eminent scientists here expresses his conviction that a new system of religious beliefs allied with science are needed at this time and that this new religion must be unified and universalized. Reading his book is a provocative experience.

LINDBERGH, CHARLES A.

Of Flight and Life. Scribner, 1948.

Acutely conscious of the extent to which the achievements of science have been perverted to destructive purposes, this unique thinker urges consideration of his own spiritual conclusions. He believes that they can be the basis of world peace.

MONSMA, JOHN CLOVER (ed.).

The Evidence of God in an Expanding Universe. Putnam, 1958.

Forty reputable scientists representing all branches of the physical and biological sciences, from mathematics and astronomy to organic chemistry and nuclear physics, here affirm their belief in the existence of a personal God.

SABINE, PAUL E.

Atoms, Men, and God. Philosophical Library, 1953.

This prominent research physicist assures us that scientific tradition accepts the corollary of a Universal Mind, and that the Mind and Thought of the Universe are of the same essence as the thought and mind of the individual.

SINNOTT, EDMUND W.

The Biology of the Spirit. Viking, 1955.

Using deductions from the findings of the biological laboratory, Dr. Sinnott has evolved an absorbing thesis in which human aspiration and the reality of the spirit of man are found imbedded in the properties of protoplasm, the basic stuff of life.

STEVENS, BERTHA.

How Miracles Abound. Illustrated. Beacon, 1941.

These lessons, emphasizing the beauty and order of the natural world, are for adults who seek to awaken children to the larger meanings of the universe. In the preface, Sophia Fahs suggests that educators who desire "to introduce into our public schools a type of education which is both religious and appropriate to a democracy may well ponder the possibilities in such a non-doctrinal education in the things of nature, such as Miss Stevens describes."

Books for Young People

Elementary

FAHS, SOPHIA.

Beginnings of Earth and Sky. Beacon, 1937.

These stories range from those based on primitive tales to those involved with modern science.

FENTON, CARROLL LANE.

Prehistoric World: Stories of Animal Life in Past Ages. Il. by the author. John Day, 1954.

This student of prehistoric life reads history in stones instead of in books and then draws and describes the snail or fish that he has become acquainted with through fossil remains.

MARCHER, MARION W.

Monarch Butterfly. Il. by Barbara Latham. Holiday House, 1954.

After reading the life story of this splendid creature, a child will want to raise one of his own. The last pages of the book tell just how this may be done.

SCHNEIDER, HERMAN and NINA.

Rocks, Rivers, and the Changing Earth. Il. by the authors. Scott, 1952.

The large type and pictures, with experiments in doing and exploring, make this a fine first book for school classes and families to read together.

SLOBODKIN, LOUIS.

Dinny and Danny. Il. by the author. Macmillan, 1951.

How would you like to have a dinosaur for a playmate? Danny found Dinny very large, of course, but he was gentle and very helpful.

STEBBING, HILARY.

Extinct Animals. Il. by the author. Penguin.

A book with big pictures in color that show how prehistoric animals looked when they were alive. It also shows their bones. Charts and a Tree of Life compare their size with that of modern animals.

WILLIAMSON, MARGARET.

The First Book of Bugs. Il. by the author. Watts, 1949.

It is good for a child to get acquainted with the insect world. If he understands the ways of bugs he is likely never to fear them.

WRIGHT, SALLY.

Gardening: A New World for Children. Il. by Ruth Sheetz. Macmillan, 1957.

The author offers stimulating ideas for starting children out on a gardening project. She tells how and when to plant and what seeds are best to choose.

Intermediate

BELL, THELMA HARRINGTON.

Snow. Il. by Corydon Bell. Viking, 1954.

The *Scientific American* called this book the "most distinguished science book for children" in the year of its publication.

FABRE, HENRI.

Insect Adventures, retold for young people by Louise Seymour Hasbrouck. Il. by Elias Goldberg. Dodd, 1919, repr. 1940.

This struggling French schoolteacher, on his small piece of waste ground, found an earthly paradise among his "pretty insects." His religious beliefs were congenial with those of his friend Maurice Maeterlinck, who is quoted at the opening of this book: "There is but one truth, whose looking-glass to our uncertain eyes seems broken, though its every fragment, whether reflecting the evolution of a planet or the flight of a bee, contains the supreme law."

GARLAND, JOSEPH, M.D.

All Creatures Here Below. Il. by René Martin. Houghton, 1954.

Dr. Garland recognizes timelessness in the developing of nature's experiments through the ages. He also sees a guiding hand—a Divinity to direct so wonderful an unfolding of life.

HOFSINDE, ROBERT.

The Indian's Secret World. Il. by the author. Morrow, 1955.

This white man with an Indian name (Gray Wolf) knows a great deal about Indian culture and thinking. He reveals many of the obscure sources of their customs.

PEATTIE, DONALD CULROSS.

The Rainbow Book of Nature. Il. by Rudolf Freund. World, 1957.

In the author's usual poetic way of looking at nature, he begins with the simplest questions that children ask. Always he invites them to observe with their own sharp eyes as unexpected marvels are pointed out.

PILKINGTON, ROGER.

In the Beginning. Il. by Piet Klaasse. St. Martin's, 1957.

The story of creation as described in the first chapters of Genesis and its amazing fulfillment in the scientific views of today are presented in this book.

REY, H. A.

Find the Constellations. Il. by the author. Houghton, 1954.

The colorful sky-views with some comic gremlins talking things over among the stars win children's interest in astronomy and take them eventually out under the night sky for their own exploring.

SANGER, MARJORY BARTLETT.

The Bird Watchers. Il. by Christine Price. Dutton, 1957.

This is the story of a family with children who have become bird-watching enthusiasts. The valuable suggestions for starting such projects make it a fine book to have when any family is acquiring a taste for bird friends.

SEAMAN, DAVID M.

The Story of Rocks and Minerals. Il. by L. Oviatt Welcome. Harvey House, 1956.

This interesting book brings with it a kit of geologic samples with which to start a small museum.

SELSAM, MILLICENT E.

Play with Seeds. Il. by Helen Ludwig. Morrow, 1957.

The origin of plants, the formation of seeds, how they travel, and other interesting subjects are discussed in this book.

Advanced

BAITY, ELIZABETH CHESLEY.

Americans before Columbus. Il. by C. B. Falls. Viking, 1951.

Mound Builders, Eskimos, Mayas, Incas, and Cave Dwellers are graphically described in this splendid book.

BAKER, ROBERT H.

When the Stars Come Out. Il. with maps and charts. Viking, rev. ed. 1954.

Luminous photographs of night skies adorn this distinguished text which contains many lessons on astronomy.

EDEL, MAY.

The Story of Our Ancestors. Il. by Herbert Danska. Little, Brown, 1955.

Bones and fossils and a timetable of geology occupy the opening chapters of this book. Then the story goes on to explore the evolution of man.

FISHER, JAMES.

The Wonderful World: The Adventure of the Earth We Live On. Art editor, F. H. K. Henrion. Hanover House, 1954.

An imaginatively conceived geography deals with the Beginning of the World, the Face of the World, and Man's World. It is illustrated with pictorial tabulations, maps, diagrams, and paintings which make it invaluable.

HOGBEN, LANCELOT.

The Wonderful World of Mathematics. Il. by Keeping and Symonds. Garden City, 1955.

A fascinating story of how civilization and mathematics developed together. Its point of view and many pictures in full color may humanize mathematics for a young student for the first time.

HOLT, RACKHAM.

George Washington Carver, an American Biography. Doubleday, 1950.

The chapters are appropriately named for Negro spirituals in the story of this eminent Negro scientist. His life was lived in the mood of the spirituals. His laboratory he called "God's Little Workshop." There, in solitary moments of communion with his Creator, he evolved his remarkable discoveries and inventions.

JESSUP, RONALD.

The Wonderful World of Archaeology. Il. by Battershill and Symonds. Garden City, 1955.

Archaeologists go into jungles and deserts, beneath the sea, and into modern laboratories to solve the mysteries of man's past. One of these scientists has given us this amazing book of his discoveries.

MAETERLINCK, MAURICE.

The Life of the Bee. New American Library, 1954.

The romantic interpretation of the orderly pattern of bee society given here sometimes makes human society seem highly experimental and clumsy.

PLATT, RUTHERFORD.

The River of Life. Il. by Bernarda Bryson. Simon and Schuster, 1956.

As an "informed amateur," the author of this book evidences a certain very attractive informality, yet is competent, through his intensive research, to discuss the whole hierarchy of living things. He does this with authority and with a contagious enthusiasm.

PLOTZ, HELEN (comp.).

Imagination's Other Place: Poems of Science and Mathematics. Il. by Clare Leighton. Crowell, 1955.

One boy, at least, found through this book that "poetry makes sense." Many another young person may learn from it to seek his own answer to the Psalmist's question, "What is man, that Thou art mindful of him?"

RAVIELLI, ANTHONY.

An Adventure in Geometry. Il. by the author. Viking, 1957.

The wonderful world of geometry in nature, "the astonishingly beautiful structure of the universe and all within," is revealed in this book with its handsome illustrations.

SCHEELE, WILLIAM E.

Prehistoric Man and the Primates. Il. by the author. World, 1957.

The director of the Cleveland Museum of Natural History has given young people a fine study of the evolution of man in this pictorial history of his development. It will be a great help to them in evaluating Darwin's *Origin of Species.*

4
SPIRITUAL INFLUENCES *in the* HOME

He took a child, and set him in the midst of them: and when he had taken him in his arms, he said unto them, Whosoever shall receive one of such children in my name, receiveth me: and whosoever shall receive me, receiveth not me, but him that sent me.

—Mark

An interpretation of religion as comprising all of life must, when applied to education, include more than school days. For education rightly begins with the dawn of consciousness in a child, and religion is deeply involved with his creation. Moreover it is during his tenderest years in the home that the foundations of his moral character must be laid.

Every living creature has started out in the same way, within the scope of a single cell. The vast potential of this microscopic unit fills one with wonder, for from it evolves a body equipped in every way. It is impossible not to see God at the heart of so great a miracle. When the mind and spirit of the human being are also considered, one exclaims involuntarily with the Psalmist, "Such knowledge is too wonderful for me; . . . I will praise thee; for I am fearfully and wonderfully made."

There is safety for the small one asleep in the egg or the womb. There is protection and warmth for it and all the sustenance needed for perfect fashioning. Each organ is developed not only in prenatal completeness but with a foresight that prepares for its functioning under conditions never to be experienced until after birth into a strange world.

Even there nature provides for the further growing time of each young thing, during which its house of life takes on a new dimension. There is infinite variety in these houses, suited as they must be to so many kinds of living. In the lower forms of life, some are found high in the air, while others are under water or in the ground. Mothers usually preside over these, though sometimes it is the male parent who takes the responsibility. Or both parents cooperate. When the period of growth, which varies from a few hours to weeks or months or longer, is completed, the creature is ready to depart and start life on its own.

But the child of man requires a much longer time to arrive at maturity—physical, mental, and spiritual. This is a slow process during which he should have two parents dedicated to his welfare, and a safe home to protect and nurture him. The home is ideally the growing-place not only of his body but of his mind and spirit as well. Within it a child should be made ready for the broader life of school and his character formed and strengthened against the day when he will have to take his own place in the world.

Home and family represent the social cell from which civilizations are born. Ever since man was man he has had some kind of home pattern and an interpretation of God which grew within it. Before temples were thought of, home was the sanctuary, in which the father was the priest and the mother the priestess. The American Indian today retains many of these traditions and makes them a part of his religion. Before he starts to build his dwelling, he first consecrates with holy rites the ground on which it will stand. Carefully he prepares the place where he will bring his articles of faith and where he can be quiet and think. Home is especially sacred to him for the reason that a new life will begin there. He believes that the breath of the Great Spirit will touch his newborn babe.

In our tradition too, man was created when God "breathed into his nostrils the breath of life." And our word "home," derived from the prehistoric word "dom," means an abiding place where one may find rest and refuge. In this fearsome atomic age, it is important to rededicate home to its primal meaning—a place where God may breathe upon His children and where we may be quiet and may think through the difficult problems of our time.

In his earliest days within the home, a child first discovers that he is something separate from others. Later he takes his place in the family group, where he should receive his first lessons in social discipline. These teach him how to live with others and how to relate himself to them, preparing him for the freedom of maturity when he will leave the security of home. The ideals and attitudes of the family deeply affect the success of this transition and all his adult life. Says one of our modern psychologists: "In recent years we have learned much about how we can, and must, help life into balance at its beginnings in childhood. We must give the child a sense of belonging. This means that we must give him the feeling that all relationships he enters are supportive. He will not then be unbalanced by fear and a sense of rejection. He will not need to turn hostile. To bring this much of balance into life is within the province of every parent or other adult within a family. . . . We do it by pursuing the ideal values that are the stuff out of which the living universe is made." [1]

This demand throws a great responsibility upon parents and other adults within a family. It reminds them that they are the teachers that teach continuously, not only by their words but by their attitudes and example. But it assumes that they themselves have been prepared for this task by having had an ideal environment at the beginning of their own lives. As a matter of fact this is seldom entirely true. Many people come ill-equipped to the time when they must accept responsibility for children, without having fully acquired the balance requisite for so delicate a task. However, it is never too late to start "pursuing the ideal values." Under the stress of necessity these may be developed satisfactorily without much early preparation. By seeking helpful friends, by affiliating themselves with constructive activities, by educating themselves through books, and by dedicating themselves to an adequate self-development, parents will find it possible to measure up to their responsibilities.

[1] Harry A. Overstreet, *The Great Enterprise.*

One of these should include the wise supervision of their children's play and the careful selection of their toys. For play habits shape ideals, and toys have a deep influence on thought patterns. This is so true that an electric train can start a railroad man on his career. A little girl's dreams of motherhood may take form while she plays with her dolls. The original incentive of a scientist may come through his first chemistry set. A box of paints can be the means of inspiring an embryo artist to a life profession. Toys have their harmful influence too, as when guns are given to children and killing games permitted. They too will be reflected in behavior patterns which just now are unfortunately conspicuous. Play should be constructive and creative. Simple toys and materials that offer an opportunity for self-expression are to be preferred to expensive toys that leave nothing to the imagination. Opportunity also for making something that seems beautiful to him should be given to every child. The expression of an original idea may come through his drawing and painting, soap-carving, block-building, and many other activities.

All the facets of family life can help in a child's personal growth. They are so numerous that it would be useless to try to touch on more than a few of them. Hospitality has been called the blessing of the home. It is surely that when each member of a family and his friends are included in it. When it expresses a wider love-among-men it comes close to being a religion. For the breaking of bread around a family table can represent a sacrament, whether the grace said over it be a Jewish or Christian prayer or a Hindu chant. Its reach can embrace a cross-section of the whole world. Entertaining should never be limited to a small circle of acquaintances, important as such intimacies are, nor restricted because of social obligation. For, to paraphrase the words of the Sermon on the Mount, "If you [entertain] only those who [entertain] you, what reward have you?" Sometimes very little. But if you go into the byways as well as the highways and bid guests from a far country or from a background different from your own, from whom you may never expect a return invitation, you are likely to have some interesting adventures in friendship. Children accustomed to this way of welcoming at home those of other backgrounds, other races and creeds, will be equipped to accept mixed classes at school and to "enter into a balanced give-and-take of life from which no one is excluded."[2] Then a universal sense of family will have been achieved and one small step in world peace taken.

In our home we carried out this idea very happily and with good results. Our guests included a great variety of people. At our Christmas dinners we always set a place for "the stranger within our gates." The rule was that it must be occupied by someone who would otherwise have no family dinner. He must never know this, however, nor feel that he was in any way a stranger, for that day he was a member of our family. Great was the rejoicing when one or another of us found such a person to invite, for, in entertaining strangers, we often found that we had entertained angels unawares. In home life, each festival can have its own tradition of sharing. The true blessing of hospitality is thus realized.

[2] Ibid.

This kind of hospitality is one way of broadening horizons. Another is by discovering a wider world outside the home. Small expeditions to museums and public buildings or even to greenhouses and stores, if introduced to them imaginatively, can be real adventures to children. If more ambitious family trips are possible, these should be discussed and mapped out in advance. Then preparations should include reading and anticipating together. Many people do not understand how important this is. I once met a family in the mission of San Juan Capistrano. The parents had wandered off with some friends, leaving their small boy alone to cope with the rather aggressive mission pigeons. He had become terrified and was throwing gravel at them. I put my arm around him and we sat down on one of the old millstones to talk. I found that he knew nothing about the mission and had no idea why he was there. It wasn't long, however, before he was absorbed in my story of the swallows and their return to San Juan Capistrano every spring on Saint Joseph's Day. We could see their nests plastered up between the arches and the baby birds' heads peeking out of them. Then I told him why the pigeons were there. In the old days, when the Indians came to the chapel services, the good padres took every means of teaching them the Christian religion. White doves were kept in wicker baskets and released from the altar during the mass. As they lighted on the Indians' heads and shoulders, the symbolism of the Holy Spirit coming down from heaven was explained. As we held corn out in our hands to the descendants of these same birds, I felt something of the same Spirit descending upon us. For the child had lost his fear, and when his parents returned they found a white dove perching on his head above a broad grin. This child could have been prepared for his visit to the mission by having Leo Politi's *Song of the Swallows* read to him. Whatever the goal of a trip may be—nature, art, scenery, history, or anything else—it is always enriched by some preparatory reading.

For that matter, appreciation of everything in life is enhanced by association with constructive home experience. If a reproduction of a good picture hangs in a child's room, how great is his rapture when he is one day shown the original. If he is taken to a concert, a sympathetic note is always struck if something is played that he has become familiar with at home. If he has developed a love of flowers in his own back yard, a tour of famous gardens takes on a special meaning.

But home has bestowed one of the richest gifts on its children if he has been introduced there to the world of books. There is no more precious experience than home reading. Whether books be read aloud in the family circle or pored over in solitude, the very first ones are never forgotten. Public circulating libraries with their vast shelves and trained librarians can be a boon in the choice of books. Yet nothing, in my opinion, can take the place of a home library, be it ever so humble. For books should be lived with, and even a very few of them can become the real center of any home. Then if each member of the family has the good fortune to possess his own personal bookcase, he may form a habit of collecting book friends that will bless him all his life. For such friends can be the greatest and wisest in all the world. "They wait until you are receptive to them; only then do they open up. First, there has to be quiet about us, peace within us; then we are ready for them. You books, truest and most silent companions, how can we thank you for your ever-present readiness, for this eternally uplifting, infinitely elevating influence of your presence! Tiny fragments of eternity, mutely ranged along an unadorned wall, you stand there unpretentiously in our home."[3]

Foremost among family books should be, of course, the Bible. It has now come down off the parlor table and is really being read. In the home, reading of the Bible can be the basis of the first lessons in religion. These should never be formal but adapted to the interests of each child in the circle. Originally religion was an accepted part of all the phases of daily life rather than something set apart and austere. I once knew a family who succeeded in keeping it so. When they came together for worship on Sundays, they all gathered in the sunny bay window of their mother's room. The canary provided the music by singing lustily. The dog usually arrived panting from a romp in the yard. There was no feeling of formality for anyone, but a gradual peace at last settled down over all. The beagle found a cool spot under the bed, where he looked out with patient eyes until he finally fell asleep. The bird always hushed his song by prayer-time and nestled his head under his wing. The reading, the discussion, and the silent prayer gave each one something very precious.

[3] Stefan Zweig, "Thanks to Books," translated by Harry Zohn, *Saturday Review*.

The sanctuary of that sunny room reflected warmth and light over experiences throughout the week and, if I am not mistaken, shone on the years ahead too.

Such family prayer-times are a good preparation for later church worship, and fortunate is the child who grows up congenially in a church home. But if organized religion does not appeal to all young people, this should not be taken to mean that they are not religious-minded, for youth is nearly always religious at heart. We should remember that fellowship and ritual are not actually essential to worship. As a matter of fact, they are only its outer forms, which must be confirmed by inner experience. Each person must, in the last analysis, stand alone in his knowledge of God. Learning the meaning of creative solitude should, therefore, be a child's first lesson in religious education. He should be taught to pray in silence, finding God within himself, and in solitude testing what is good or bad in his conduct toward others. Then his experience of religion will take on a new dimension. When, in maturity, the time comes for him to leave his home and go into the world, he will take with him an abiding sanctuary and an unfailing Companion to guide him as the problems of life come upon him. The early establishing of such spiritual security is the richest legacy that any home can bestow upon its children.

READING LISTS

ARBUTHNOT, MAY HILL.

Children and Books. Scott Foresman, 1947.

This "parent's guide to children's reading" is an expert's answer to those who wonder about the choice of books for children from two years through junior high.

BRO, MARGUERITE HARMON.

When Children Ask. Harper, rev. ed. 1956.

An intelligent treatise on how to answer, not merely reply to, children's questions. A solid basis for spiritual education in the home.

DREIKURS, RUDOLPH.

The Challenge of Parenthood. Duell, 1948.

A psychiatrist looks at parenthood and helpfully analyzes its many problems.

DUFF, ANNIS.

"Bequest of Wings": A Family's Pleasures with Books. Viking, 1944.

"Longer Flight": A Family Grows Up with Books. Viking, 1955.

These delightful books belong together as they follow the sequences of a family's growing up together—socially, intellectually, and spiritually.

GAER, JOSEPH.

The Bible for Family Reading. Little, Brown, 1956.

A concisely organized arrangement of the Bible for easy reading. The language approximates the Authorized Version but with obscurities and archaisms eliminated.

JONES, RUFUS.

Finding the Trail of Life. Macmillan, 1943.

An intimate interpretation of his own spiritual growth in boyhood by this great Quaker who was so eminently successful in finding his trail of life.

MARSHALL, CATHERINE and PETER.

God Loves You. Whittlesey, 1953.

Bible selections, prayers, and stories used by the Marshall family who made religion a vital part of daily living.

PARENTS' COOPERATIVE GROUP.

The Challenge of Children. Morrow, 1958.

Ten parents wrote this book together as a cooperative venture. Demanding maturity and understanding, they promise parents the reward of mutual awareness in the child-parent relationship if they meet their responsibilities intelligently.

PARENTS, FOR PARENTS BY.

The World from Our Home. Pam. Friendship, 1956.

The importance of developing world understanding in the home is here emphasized and suggestions made for learning its techniques through books, music, and worship.

RAYNOLDS, ROBERT.

The Choice to Love. Harper, 1959.

Because it is on love that home and family are founded and maintained, I offer parents this collection of wise essays written by a well-known novelist who calls it "a book of a man at his hearth and in his home."

SHUTTLESWORTH, DOROTHY EDWARDS.

Exploring Nature with Your Child. Greystone, 1952.

An introduction to the enjoyment of many fields of nature for all the family. It is full of the fascinating facts that children want to know about creatures and plants.

THURMAN, HOWARD.

The Creative Encounter. Harper, 1954.

I am introducing this book, in this chapter, particularly for Dr. Thurman's discussion of "The Inner Need of Love," though there are riches on every page of his book.

TRENT, ROBBIE.

Your Child and God. Harper, 1952.

Many questions regarding the spiritual development of children are discussed here with great insight. It is a book to be highly recommended to parents who crave for their children a sound basis for faith and understanding.

TRUEBLOOD, ELTON and PAULINE.

The Recovery of Family Life. Harper, 1953.

The Truebloods, who are leaders in the Quaker faith, have dedicated this book to their own family, which is a good indication that it has something for yours.

WALTERS, ZELIA M.

You and Your Child. Lee's Summit, Mo.: Unity School, 1950.

Mrs. Walters writes for fathers and mothers from a "Truth" standpoint. She lays down no fixed rules for directing children in spiritual growth, knowing that every child requires a different plan. Yet by giving examples from her own experience with children, she advises on ways of meeting the common problems that arise all the way from babyhood to adolescence.

5
FINDING AESTHETIC *and* SPIRITUAL VALUES *in* LITERATURE

He is my self within the heart, smaller than a corn of rice, smaller than a corn of barley, smaller than a mustard seed, smaller than a canary seed, or the kernel of a canary seed. He also is my self, within the heart, greater than the earth, greater than the sky, greater than heaven, greater than all these worlds.

—*Upanishads*

The printed word is the silent vehicle that carries thoughts from one mind to another. When a child learns to read, there is opened up into his consciousness a vast highway. Over this an ever-increasing stream of ideas of all kinds will apply for entrance. Cultivation of a discriminating taste for what is worthy is one of our important duties to young people, for this will protect them from what is undesirable in literature, and in life. We must find and present to them books that will give them knowledge, pleasure, and inspiration.

In spiritual education sacred books might seem to be the natural choice. But all good books are, in a way, sacred, and there are plenty of spiritual overtones in secular literature. In this chapter I give examples that show this to be true. Symbolic fairy and folk tales, distilled as they have been through many generations of telling, are loaded with insight and wisdom. Their moral implications make them fundamental to the kind of religious philosophy we are discussing.

Tales such as "Beauty and the Beast," "Red Riding Hood," "Cinderella," and many others are basic to our literary tradition. These were originally intended for adults, but they have always appealed to children, who have adopted them for their own. Each story has depths of thought beneath its enchanting narrative. "The Sleeping Beauty" is an allegory of human love. The love of the Good Fairy, whose interception neutralizes a curse on the Princess, is a symbol of idealized human friendship. The fostering love of the King and Queen for their daughter is the natural yearning of all good parents toward their children. Finally the romantic love of the Prince, who wakes the sleeping Princess and all her world with a kiss, typifies the hope everyone has of joining love to love and living happily ever after.

In such tales "a quality in things, an atmosphere larger than life is created. In their reading of fairy tales children are persuaded that 'unselfish and faithful love always ends by finding its reward, be it only in oneself,' and they discover 'how ugly and low are jealousy and greed.' And these are some of the things that children want to know. Through the succession of clear mental pictures a child sees that even the weakest can be more than a match for the evil and ugly things in the world if he possess courage, quick wits, and a good heart—a useful and sustaining reflection for anyone in a world as alarming as our own."[1]

We must help those who are growing up in this world to understand the language of spirit. "God, for us, is the great spirit of Love from Whom all the love of fathers and mothers comes; God, for us, is Infinite All-being, incomprehensible, yet not unknowable; God, for us, is the Father and Mother-Soul of the universe. Is there risk in using fairy stories to draw the child nearer to the thought of God? Not, I believe, if we ourselves are conscious, as we tell them, of the deep, underlying truth of fairy lore. In early childhood, the abstract must needs be clothed in the concrete; and gradually, if we do not misinterpret, if we have told such stories in the right way, the children will cast off the husk, retaining the kernel—and still understand. The romance of fairies, gnomes, and sprites is full of spiritual truth. Everything around us has a spirit of its own, is fraught with mystery. Natural objects are thoughts of the Creative Power clothed in matter.[2]

The most important fairy tale to come out of our present age is *Alice's Adventures in Wonderland*. It is in fact one of the outstanding books of all time. Recently presented to the people of England, the original manuscript now rests in the British Museum. The reason for the universal recognition of this "little book," as the author called it, is the profound philosophy planted in its enchanting whimsy. Another book which has attained the place of a classic for the same reason is *At the Back of the North Wind*. Little Diamond, its hero,

[1] Lilian H. Smith, *The Unreluctant Years.*
[2] Elizabeth Mumford, *The Dawn of Religion.*

was a boy "given to metaphysics." He possessed the secret of life, and was himself what he was so ready to think the lowest living thing—an angel of God with something special to say or do. "I cannot pretend to account for it," says the author, "I leave that for each philosophical reader to do after his own fashion." [3]

Some people are surprised to find such philosophical readers in the lower age brackets. Not so Margaret Wise Brown (Golden MacDonald). She never wrote down to youngsters, but in simple stories, suited to their time of life, she wrapped up some very profound thoughts for small children. *The Little Island* shows how truth is revealed in the secret depths of silence. It also deals with the mystery of personal identity and its relationship with society and with God. An older philosopher gives authority to the moral of this fable. "William James invoked the hypothesis of a subliminal connection between the individual's mind and the universal mind. The island of individual consciousness, to use his analogy, rests ultimately upon the limitless ocean floor from which it draws its composition and support." [4]

This little Island knew that it was both a "part of the world, and a world of its own, all surrounded by the bright blue sea." Neither was it to be shaken out of this conviction by a pert young kitten.

"I am part of this big world," said the kitten. "My feet are on it."

"So am I," said the little Island.

[3] George Macdonald, *At the Back of the North Wind.*
[4] Gordon W. Allport, *The Individual and His Religion.*

"No you're not," said the kitten. "Water is all around you and cuts you off from the land."

"Ask any fish," said the Island.

So the kitten caught a fish. "Answer me this or I'll eat you up," said the kitten. "How is an island a part of the land?"

"Come with me," said the fish, "down into the dark secret places of the sea and I will show you."

"I can't swim," said the cat. "Show me another way or I'll eat you up."

"Then you must take it on faith what I tell you," said the fish.

"What's that?" said the cat—"Faith."

"To believe what I tell you about what you don't know," said the fish. And the fish told the kitten how all land is one land under the sea. The cat's eyes were shining with the secret of it. And because he loved secrets he believed.[5]

Is it because they love secrets that faith comes so naturally to children? Or is it because their imaginations are so keen that they really understand "the evidence of things not seen"? Whatever the source of a child's faith, we must do all we can to nurture it. For faith surmounts fear, it comforts in the secret places of the heart, it opens windows toward heaven through which it is possible to talk with God. Seek out passages in literature that describe it as natural and beautiful, and give them to children.

"See that rose that the candle is shedding its light on? It bloomed in faith, opening its petals to sun and rain, wind and night, knowing it would be cared for through them all. Do you think God could care for the rose and not for you?"[6] "Look at the stars above you. Look long enough, and you

[5] Golden MacDonald, *The Little Island.*
[6] Elizabeth Yates, *Patterns on the Wall.*

will see God's bright host. 'He shall give his angels charge over thee.' It's promised. Balm of faith! The night was a tall mansion, curtained with sleep, with silence."[7]

In biography children may find many good companions who have experienced the faith they know about. Elizabeth Janet Gray lets us listen with her to the early whisperings in the heart of one of these: "Young William Penn had much to think about. . . . Alone in his room one day, he had a strange experience. Suddenly he knew there was a God, not because people said so in church, but because he knew it within his own heart. He felt as if God Himself were telling him so, and for a fleeting moment the room seemed to be filled with a holy light, and he felt comforted. It was gone almost at once. He did not speak of it to anyone. Sometimes for long periods he did not even think of it, but he never quite forgot it. Years later he knew what it meant."[8] By reading his life, we too may know what it meant, this abiding faith—patience in prison, heroism in the face of persecution, courage for exploring an unknown continent, and wisdom for founding a colony on brotherly love.

What of this love of all mankind which so closely approaches the love of God? It is to be found shining in prisons and palaces, in people of high intellectual attainments as well as in such untutored souls as Johnny Appleseed. "Before ever he had begun to plant orchards on the frontier, Johnny had taken up a new faith. Perhaps he did not understand the whole of it, but in his own way, he made use of the

[7] Mabel Leigh Hunt, *Better Known as Johnny Appleseed.*
[8] Elizabeth Janet Gray, *Penn.*

heart of it. And the heart of it was love—the love of God for man, and of man for God—love of all creation in a universe wherein the spiritual world is as real as that lesser one in which we move. Love for all creation—it was as simple as that for simple-hearted Johnny."[9]

Said a child I knew whose spirit had an unusual inner flowering, perhaps because outwardly he was slow of speech and spastic of body, "This is God's earth we are on. Why did He put us here? Because so that we could discover what love is." Knowing love is as important as breathing pure air or eating wholesome food, yet discernment of its true meaning often has to wait upon some special quickening of the imagination. This may come through suffering, as it probably did for this boy.

Another child, this one speaking from the pages of a book, describes the way such understanding came to him. He suffered because his growing-up seemed so slow and his elders so lacking in appreciation of him. In desperation he turned at last to his patron saint. He asked the saint to arrange things more happily for him. It was a selfish prayer, but it eventually opened up to him an experience of truer love for his brother and a deeper reverence for God. Later on he improved his prayer:

"San Ysidro. Dear Sir. This is Miguel Chavez who took up so much of your time last year and I have no complaints. Thank you for last year. But this year I haven't got a wish. No wish at all. All I wish, San Ysidro, is for things to be the way you wish. Amen."

[9] Hunt, op. cit.

"That's a good prayer," said his brother, "but didn't I hear something like it before? It sounded like 'Our Father' didn't it? Thy will be done on earth as it is in heaven. Amen."[10]

John Bowman describes his own childhood conflicts and a dawn of prayer in another idiom. Of one of his crises he writes: "I hurried to the yard, out to the garden, and down between two long rows of raspberry bushes. Near the far end and where the bushes were thickest I hid under a clump. The grass was good to sit on, I was alone and glad of it. There was so much to think about that it was hard to get started. Something had to be done. You had to make a choice in this world. You could step on toward paradise and be large and kind like God, or you could hang by the hair like Absalom and die. There was no middle way. It was time that I say what I would do. I had heard of saints but I did not know about them. I did know about poets. They made you feel things and did good. They were, of all people, most like God; they talked about birds and trees and what everybody knew; they had their birthdays remembered. One thing was plain. I would be a poet. I could never tell; I would just begin."[11]

This boy's answer came clear to him apparently because his father had made a practice of reading to him from the poets. Poetry was a reality to him when all else seemed nebulous. There is always a chance that giving children art in any form may have some far-reaching effects. We never know what hearing good music may do for a potential musician, or how exposure to great painting and sculpture may

[10] Joseph Krumgold, *And Now Miguel.*
[11] John G. Bowman, *The World That Was.*

shape the imaginings of an artist in embryo. And art goes hand in hand with philosophy and religion.

So it did in the poetry of Wordsworth. In his "Lines Composed a Few Miles Above Tintern Abbey" he describes the ecstasy of his youth with some nostalgia. But then goes on to say:

> Not for this
> Faint I, nor mourn nor murmur; other gifts
> Have followed; for such loss, I would believe,
> Abundant recompense. For I have learned
> To look on nature, not as in the hour
> Of thoughtless youth; but hearing oftentimes
> The still, sad music of humanity,
> Nor harsh nor grating, though of ample power
> To chasten and subdue. And I have felt
> A presence that disturbs me with the joy
> Of elevated thoughts: a sense sublime
> Of something far more deeply interfused,
> Whose dwelling is the light of setting suns,
> And the round ocean and the living air,
> And the blue sky, and in the mind of man:
> A motion and a spirit, that impels
> All thinking things, all objects of all thought,
> And rolls through all things.

The skill of the flyer gave yet another dimension to the art of Antoine St. Exupéry. He also reached back into his boyhood, when he wrote *The Little Prince*. In it he describes an encounter in the desert with what may have been his subconscious mind. He begins by telling realistically that he had "made a forced landing in the Sahara alone, a thousand miles from help," and with water enough for only a few days. Then follows the fantasy of his meeting with that "extraordinary small person" whom we can only take to be his alter ego. From his poignant narrative is distilled an exquisite philosophy:

> It is much more difficult to judge oneself than to judge others. If you succeed in judging yourself rightly, then you are indeed a man of true wisdom. . . . It is only with the heart that one can see rightly; what is essential is invisible to the eye. Men have forgotten this truth, but you must not forget it. . . . All men have the stars, but they are not the same things for different people. You—you alone—will have the stars as no one else has them. In one of the stars I shall be living. Tonight do not come. I shall look as if I were dead and that will not be true. You understand. . . . I cannot carry this body with me. It is too heavy. But it will be like an old abandoned shell. There is nothing sad about old shells. You know, it will be very nice. I, too, shall look at the stars. All the stars will pour out fresh water for me to drink.[12]

Death must enter into a child's religion, for it is a part of life. But it must come as a symbol, perhaps the only way it should be interpreted by anyone—as a "parched leaf falling in its time," [13] as a "white gull, with wings to fly hither and yon where it wills," [14] as a snowflake becoming "a part of the vast, silent spaces of the heavens," [15] as tulips in our flower bed that "all winter God remembers," [16] and as the seed "it

[12] Antoine de St. Exupéry, *The Little Prince.*
[13] Felix Salten, *Bambi.*
[14] Ruth Sawyer, *Roller Skates.*
[15] Paul Gallico, *The Snowflake.*
[16] Jessie Orton Jones, *Secrets.*

may chance of wheat, or of some other grain . . . which . . . is not quickened, except it die" (I Corinthians 15:36–37).

In every creature, in forest and ocean, in leaf and tree and bird and beast and man, there moves a spirit other than his mortal own, . . .
And this is the spirit of immortality and peace,
And whatsoever creature hath this spirit, to it no harm may befall:
No harm can befall, for wherever it goes it has its nested home, and to it every loss comes charged with an equal gain;
It gives—but to receive a thousand-fold;
It yields its life—but at the hands of love;
And death is the law of its eternal growth.
And I saw that was the law of every creature . . .
And wherever it penetrated, behold! there was nothing left, down to the smallest atom, which was not a winged spirit instinct with life.[17]

[17] Carpenter, *Towards Democracy.*

READING LISTS

BEVAN, EDWYN ROBERT.

Symbolism and Belief. Beacon, 1957.

To those interested in a broad study of symbolism I recommend these Gifford Lectures given by a British scholar from King's College, London.

BOWMAN, JOHN G.

The World That Was. Rutgers University, 1947.

A great educator gives here an intimate reminiscence of his childhood, which was a delightful magical lifetime filled with trees, grass, sky, rocks, and cats, and at the same time tempered with considerable anguish.

CLARK, GLENN.

God's Voice in the Folklore. Il. by Marcia Brown. Saint Paul, Minnesota: Macalester Park Publishing Co., 1956.

Just as material riches are to be found in the depths of the earth, so treasures of truth and wisdom lie hidden in folklore. An intuitive spiritual leader has mined some of these for us and interpreted them in this book.

EATON, ANNE THAXTER.

Treasure for the Taking. Viking, rev. ed. 1957.

This compilation of booklists in revised edition is more than ever an indispensable guide to discovery of books to delight and enlighten children of all ages.

HARPER, RALPH.

The Sleeping Beauty. Harper, 1955.

Within the framework of a fairy tale, the author discusses, with reference to various philosophical thought and with an insight all his own, the elusive sense of "presence" experienced in art, in love, in nature, and in prayer.

HAZARD, PAUL.

Books, Children, and Men. Horn Book, 1948.

A distinguished and much traveled French man-of-letters has given us this classic dealing with children's literature. He asks that children's books share with their readers deep emotions, building respect for universal life and for the mysterious in creation and in man.

SAWYER, RUTH.

The Way of the Storyteller. Viking, 1942.

A remarkable storyteller shares her rich experience and joy in her art and tells eleven of her best-loved stories.

STEFFERUD, ALFRED (ed.).

The Wonderful World of Books. Il. by Robert Osborn. New American Library, 1953.

This valuable book is dedicated "to those who bend twigs and to the twigs themselves" by the book people who contributed so generously to producing it.

Books for Young People

Elementary

DE ANGELI, MARGUERITE.

Book of Nursery and Mother Goose Rhymes. Il. by the author. Doubleday, 1953.

A beautiful book for introducing these loved rhymes to little folks.

DICKENS, CHARLES.

The Magic Fishbone; a Romance from the Pen of Miss Alice Rainbird. Il. by Louis Slobodkin. Vanguard, 1954.

A good introduction to what may prove a lifetime of pleasure with Dickens. Also a possible inducement to other young misses to try their hands at romance.

DONAHEY, MARY DICKERSON.

The Castle of Grumpy Grouch. Il. by Pelagie Doane. Random, 1948.

This lively tale which has pleased young readers for two generations has to do with a princess, gypsies, witches, fairies, and animals who talk. Its moral is simple.

GOULDER, SHIRLEY, retold by.

Tales from Hans Andersen. Il. by Maraja. Grosset.

The Sleeping Beauty and Other Tales (Perrault). Il. by Benvenuti. Grosset.

These two books offer great tales for children to grow on. Their colors are so glowing that it seems they must have absorbed some of the sunshine of Italy, where they were produced.

JONES, JESSIE ORTON.

Secrets. Il. by Elizabeth Orton Jones. Viking, 1945.

Like an iceberg, the greater part of a book is often below the surface. This simple text is supported by psychological and religious truths.

LAWSON, ROBERT.

Rabbit Hill. Il. by the author. Viking, 1944.

This amusing story of a clan of greedy rabbits ends with a little sermon when they come upon a statue of St. Francis with water dripping from his hands for all the birds and small animals to drink and with the motto "There is enough for all."

MOTHER GOOSE.

Seventy-seven Verses. Il. by Tasha Tudor. Oxford, 1944.

These lilting rhymes never fail to please small readers nor do this artist's pictures.

Nursery Tales, The Tall Book of. Il. by Feodor Rojankovsky. Harper, 1944.

These stories have been in the bloodstream of our culture for generations and should always be continued. The illustrations are, of course, distinguished.

THURBER, JAMES.

Many Moons. Il. by Louis Slobodkin. Harcourt, 1943.

Every child will love this fable of a little princess who wanted the moon, while grown-ups will find entertainment in its tongue-in-cheek humor.

WEISGARD, LEONARD.

Who Dreams of Cheese? Il. by the author. Scribner, 1950.

Dreams are for children and little animals, sometimes asleep and sometimes awake—all tender, all intimately suggestive of natural and wholesome longings.

WERNER, ELSA JANE.

Giant Golden Book of Elves and Fairies. Il. by Garth Williams. Simon and Schuster, 1951.

Literally an enchanting book with assorted pixies, mermaids, brownies, witches, and leprechauns all painted in this artist's most imaginative style.

Finding Aesthetic and Spiritual Values in Literature

Intermediate

BARRIE, JAMES M.

Peter Pan. Il. by Nora S. Unwin. Scribner, 1950.

The Never-Never Land of Peter and the visit to it by a few small mortals will ever be one of the best loved of all modern fairy tales. The artist brings to it her own particular magic.

DE LA MARE, WALTER.

Come Hither. Il. by Warren Chappell. Knopf, 1957.

A rare anthology of poetry for the young of all ages with an introduction and commentary by one of the best of all poets.

FARJEON, ELEANOR.

The Glass Slipper. Il. by Ernest H. Shepard. Viking, 1956.

This version of the Cinderella story is beautifully told by an illustrious writer and pictured by one of the best-loved artists.

FERRIS, HELEN (comp.).

Favorite Poems Old and New. Il. by Leonard Weisgard. Doubleday, 1957.

These 700 poems represent a careful selection of the best. Illustrations by Leonard Weisgard always glorify a book.

FROST, WILLIAM HENRY.

The Wagner Story Book. Il. by Sydney Burleigh. Scribner, 1894.

I have found this old book to be most discerning of the hidden meanings in Wagner's music dramas. If it is not easily obtainable in libraries, I urge parents and teachers to search for other books that will give children the moral lessons taught in the Niebelungenlied.

GRIMM, THE BROTHERS.

Tales from Grimm. Trans. and il. by Wanda Gág. Coward-McCann, 1936.

More Tales from Grimm. Trans. and il. by Wanda Gág. Coward-McCann, 1947.

Few understand Grimm quite so well as this delightful interpreter of his tales.

GORDON, PATRICIA.

The Oldest Secret. Il. by Garry MacKenzie. Viking, 1953.

Between the lines of his textbook, Hugh found the Back of Beyond, a dream which came true on an enchanted island. There he met so many book characters that this book would qualify as a textbook of literature.

HERSHOLT, JEAN (trans.).

Andersen's Fairy Tales. Il. by Fritz Kredel. Heritage, 1952.

It seems fitting that a Dane should translate these tales and that an artist from not-so-far-away Frankfort who understands them so well should illustrate them.

JONES, ELIZABETH ORTON.

Twig. Il. by the author. Macmillan, 1942.

With enough imagination, a little girl living in a very drab tenement might find fairyland in her own back yard. Twig was able to do this and so discovered the secret of magic in everything that happened in her little world.

LANG, ANDREW (ed.).

The Blue Fairy Book. Il. by Ben Kutcher. Longmans, 1949.

Children of today love these old tales that have pleased so many generations.

LOVE, KATHERINE (comp.).

A Little Laughter. Il. by Walter H. Lorraine. Crowell, 1957.

Poetry can be lighthearted as well as serious. This is a gay anthology covering a wide range of choice.

Advanced

ADSHEAD, GLADYS L., and DUFF, ANNIS (comps.).

An Inheritance of Poetry. Il. by Nora S. Unwin. Houghton, 1948.

This book is introduced with a quotation from the Apocrypha (Maccabees 2:25): "We have been careful that they that read may have delight." Every reader must agree that these editors have been most successful in their purpose.

ANDERSEN, HANS CHRISTIAN.

It's Perfectly True, and Other Stories. Trans. by Paul Leyssac. Il. by Richard Bennett. Harcourt, 1938.

A Danish actor and author, whose mother had actually listened to Andersen telling them, has appropriately translated these best-loved stories.

BECKER, MAY LAMBERTON.

First Adventures in Reading. Lippincott, rev. ed. 1954.

To teen-age people, young adults, who are forming their opinions of books, this sympathetic discussion, with its reading lists, is addressed.

BRO, MARGUERITE HARMON.

Let's Talk About You. Doubleday, 1945.

This wise author tells teen-agers that their happiness depends on getting the most out of life by deciding first what is most important to them, and then by living close to their ideals.

FROST, ROBERT.

You Come Too: Favorite Poems for Young Readers. Il. by Thomas W. Nason. Holt, 1959.

These poems were chosen for you by the poet himself. After being introduced to him by Hyde Cox and reading the poems all through, you may find that you, too, have made a lifelong friend of this great American.

GODDEN, RUMER.

In Noah's Ark. Viking, 1949.

Allusive, comic, startlingly colloquial at times, yet filled with passages of lyrical beauty and intensity, this poem creates a new and delightful myth out of the eternal legend of the Flood.

PLOTZ, HELEN (comp.).

Untune the Sky: Poems of Music and the Dance. Il. by Clare Leighton. Crowell, 1957.

The essence of music and the dance, as well as the rhythm of the illustrations make this compilation unusual and very choice.

SHAKESPEARE, WILLIAM.

A Midsummer's Night's Dream. Dutton, 1936.

The Tempest. Dutton, 1936.

In both these plays the involvement of human affairs with supernatural forces is symbolically illustrated.

SAINT EXUPÉRY, ANTOINE DE.

The Little Prince. Il. by the author. Reynal & Hitchcock, 1923.

Before becoming quite grown up is the best time to understand the mystic implications of this book. If you miss them then, you may have to wait under your star for a long time to learn what is really important.

6

The PLACE *of* WORLD RELIGIONS *in* EDUCATION

Your God is One God.
He it is Who created for you all that is in the earth.
The East and the West is God's:
Therefore, whichever way ye turn, there is the face of God.

—*Koran*

Brotherhood, at this time, which may well be a turning point in history, includes not only family and nation but the whole human race. To keep the peace spiritually, economically, and politically in so extensive a relationship represents a very real challenge. It demands acquaintance with all our brothers. For that reason, the study of cultural patterns is an important part of education today. As these patterns stem largely from religious traditions, the history and literature of world religions should be included. Each one of them brings its own interpretation of worship and morality, and all have something to contribute to the understanding between peoples. Says Charles Lindbergh: "To progress, even to survive, we must learn to apply the truths of God to the actions and relationships of men. . . . We must learn from the sermons of Christ, the wisdom of Laotzu, the teachings of Buddha. In these, in the Bible of the Hebrews, in the philosophy of Greece, in the Indian Vedas, in the writings of saints and mystics, we have a record of the great religious and moral truths discovered by man through the ages at his moments of highest inspiration. Our mission is to understand these truths, to separate them from the dogma which surrounds them, and to apply them to our way of life." [1]

It is also our mission to present, without prejudice, these great religious and moral truths to children. First we must cultivate, in them and in ourselves, an attitude of openness toward ways other than our own. Something beyond tolerance must be sought. I saw a simple example of this once when we were going through Chinatown. There were two schoolboys ahead of us as we approached a shrine in the Joss House. I heard one of them say to the other, "Take off your hat! Can't you see this is somebody's God?" That was true tolerance, and reverence too.

It is not hard to explain to young people that the outer aspects of religious rites and ceremonies are sure to be different, just as races are different. The forms and creeds, sacred books, objects, and metaphors revered by people vary greatly. Also an overlay of superstition is likely to obscure their true significance and separate people by surface misunderstandings. But at the still center of each, it will be found that all religions contain elements of Absolute Truth, and for that

[1] *Of Flight and Life.*

reason they are basically congenial. At that level, let us introduce young people to the universality of this Truth.

All great religions strive to find the Principle behind the universe and to apply it to human problems. One dominant Rule appears in most of them. We call it the Golden Rule. It is the admonition to treat others as we ourselves would have them treat us. It is for all people everywhere who would walk the way of peace. An interesting project for a schoolroom would be to seek out these various Golden Rules and to compare them. Another would be to discover symbolic words used in common to express spiritual meaning. For instance, the "Word" used by John to describe the intangible creative Force in the universe can be translated broadly into the Chinese "Tao," back into the Greek "Logos" from which it came, and into the "Word in the Supreme Heaven" of the Upanishads. They are almost synonymous. Isaiah makes a transition to another word in "Thine ears shall hear a word behind thee saying, This is the way, walk ye in it." The "Way" also described the early Christian doctrine. Then the "noble Path" of Buddhism, and the Moslem "Path of thy Lord," and Zoroaster's "upward Path of Asha" are but one step further.

Working together on this kind of symbolism in classes should help to meet the problem of religious prejudice which has troubled many schools. Also tensions might be alleviated by learning about the religious festivals celebrated in a community and even taking part in them. They need not conflict, but rather should enrich one another. The traditions of the Christmas season could appropriately be celebrated in schools of mixed races by observing both the Christian Nativity and the Feast of Lights of the Jews. This more ancient festival is marked by the lighting of candles symbolizing the passing of the winter darkness and the new birth of light in the world. These beautiful lines describe some of its implications:

A candle is a small thing,
But one candle can light another;
And as it gives its flame to the other,
See how its own light increases.
You are such a light.
You have the power to move back the darkness in yourself and in others—with the birth of light when one mind illuminates another, when one heart kindles another, when one man strengthens another.[2]

The Jewish harvest-time, Sukkoth, with its week of tabernacled worship, is a feast of greater religious import than our Puritan Thanksgiving seems now to be. Saint Patrick's Day has become almost a national holiday and a very popular one. There are other Catholic saints' days too, that might well be generally observed. In the full moon of May, the Oriental Wesak picturesquely commemorates the birth, death, and enlightenment of Gautama Buddha. This is one of many rites celebrated near the time of the Christian Easter. All these religious festivals offer splendid material for assembly programs which can be designed to contribute to the religious integration of a school.

After being given general preparation for the understanding of various religions, pupils are ready to study their his-

[2] Hanukka message of the Jewish Theological Seminary of America.

tories and literatures. All religions have their beguiling fables and myths, and the lives of their founding prophets are usually wonderous tales. The founder of Taoism is a legendary person to be approached with great reverence. It is supposed that he was born in China centuries before Christ, "in the village known as Good Man's Bend, in the Thistle District of Bramble Province."[3] He is said to have been born old, with white hair, and so has always been called Lao-Tse or Old Boy. His knowledge of books was fabulous and his fame for wisdom spread throughout the world. It is small wonder then that Confucius, the Perfect Sage, made a pilgrimage to consult this venerable Old Philosopher. If he had hoped for soft answers to his queries, however, he was disappointed, for the aging Wise One told him sharply to leave off his proud airs and to get free of all show and fuss. Afterward Confucius said to his disciples, "I know how the birds fly, how fishes swim, how animals run. But there is the Dragon. Today I have seen the Dragon. My mouth was agape: I could not shut it."[4] Lao-Tse became more and more impatient with what seemed to him the insincerities in the people of China and decided to run away. The gate-keeper saw him going through the gate of the city and begged him to return. So he went back and stayed until he had written the *Tao Te king* which one may say means "Canon of Reason-Path-Word-Nature-God-Virtue."[5] After this he mounted a water buffalo and rode into the West where "it was believed there

[3] Sheldon Cheney, *Men Who Have Walked with God.*
[4] Robert O. Ballou, ed., *The Portable World Bible.*
[5] Ibid.

was a realm where sages lived under conditions surviving from the Golden Age, where rules and rulers were unknown, and where life was not interrupted by the change called death."[6]

The Book of Tao is a profound book and also a very simple one. In it Lao-Tse tells children that "the Way is not too great for the smallest."[7] It may be that the little ones will understand his philosophy best.

> In all the earth nothing weaker than water.
> Yet in attacking the hard, nothing superior.
> Nothing so certain in wearing down strength:
> There is no way to resist it.
> Note then: The weak conquer the strong,
> The yielding outlast the aggressors.
>
> * * *
>
> The wheel's hub holds thirty spokes:
> Utility depends on the hole through the hub.
>
> * * *
>
> The potter's clay forms a vessel:
> It is the space within that serves.
>
> * * *
>
> A house is built with solid walls:
> The nothingness of window and door
> Alone renders it usable.

This sage of China teaches "if one become quiet, unassertive, inconspicuous, empty, that one may be filled with God."[8]

This was a very different philosophy from that developed

[6] Cheney, op. cit.
[7] Ballou, *The Bible of the World*.
[8] Cheney, op. cit.

by Confucius, who tried in vain to learn something from it. He was a practical man, serving first as chief magistrate and finally as minister of justice in his province. During the time of his service it became almost a model state. But, as often happens to successful men, he was attacked by jealous rivals and eventually banished. Whether his greatest contributions were made during his prosperity in one province or in the days when he wandered throughout all China seeking employment it is hard to say. Somewhere along the way, he was able to edit the old sacred writings of China and to establish their authority, which is respected to this day. Upon them he founded a religion which excels in ethics designed for daily living. His words were taken down by faithful disciples during his lifetime and collected in the famous *Analects*. After his death he was canonized and repeatedly honored as a saint. Finally the Empress Dowager raised him to the rank of deity of Heaven and Earth.

No great prophet appears in the Hindu religion, perhaps the oldest one that we know about. Its antecedents can be traced into a most remote past, when the Aryans invaded the Indian peninsula and brought with them their primitive gods. Their rituals were elaborate and an extensive literature developed around them. More than a hundred books, including those called the *Vedas,* are still preserved.

There was eventual reaction to what became a complicated system of worship as the Aryans penetrated deeper into India. Their gods multiplied as their race began to mix with the brown natives they found there. Lest they lose their racial identity entirely, an elaborate caste system was worked out which still persists in some degree. However, this did not prevent a fusion of the two races. Today the people of India have Aryan characteristics but dark skins. Their religion has been simplified into one dominated by the One Absolute Brahma, Principle of Creation. In spite of his apparent Allness, Vishnu who preserves and Shiva who destroys, are also worshiped. Of all these Vishnu is the most popular for he is especially solicitous toward human beings. In fact, as an agent of God, it is believed that he often comes to earth in various incarnations to minister to them. From this belief has developed a literature rich in revelation and wonderful tales. The *Mahabharata* is an account of the incarnation of Vishnu in the hero Krishna. He in turn impersonates a charioteer in that gem of ethical discussion called the *Bhagavad-Gita,* the *Song Celestial.* Vishnu was also incarnated in Rama, hero of the epic poem the *Ramayana.* For teaching, and for learning, these two magnificent epics are splendid material.

American children are fortunate in having had an emissary from India to bring them, in their own language, stories from his country. Dhan Gopal Mukerji was born a Brahman and undertook the hardships of pilgrimage and temple service at an early age. One day his Holy Man said to him, "Do you know, if you could play with the Lord, perhaps it would be the biggest thing that has ever been done. Everybody takes Him so seriously that they make Him dull as death. Away with rituals; go, play with the Lord!" [9] This advice may offer something to our own program of religious education. It seems to have influenced the young Gopal in an un-

[9] Dhan Gopal Mukerji, *Caste and Outcast.*

expected way, for he tells us that about that time he was convinced that religion no longer spelled priesthood to him. Renouncing his caste, he came to America at eighteen to enter the university at Berkeley, California. His life in this country was dedicated to reconciling the East and the West. One of the means he used was giving to the "Christian reader the word of God as revealed to the Hindu race." [10] Another was writing books for our Western children to show them the everyday life of his people and the early spiritual training given to children in India.

We were blessed in having Mukerji for our personal friend. We enjoyed listening to his stories as he told them around our fireside. His books taught us the meaning of silence and the place of meditation in worship. We knew the prayer of his jungle lad:

> Reveal to us the face of God,
> Whose shadow is this day, and
> Whose light is always within us.
> Lead us from the unreal to the Real,
> From darkness unto Light, and
> From sound into Silence.[11]

When Mukerji first came to our house, we wanted to be able to show him our appreciation of his books. As I prepared our lunch, the children drew their chairs close to his and kept the silence they felt would refresh him before his afternoon talk at the school. Afterwards he often laughingly said that the greatest wonder he had beheld in this country

[10] Mukerji, *Devotional Passages.*
[11] Mukerji, *Kari the Elephant.*

was two American children keeping still for fifteen minutes!

Turning to Buddhism, we find the story of its founder is the story of a prince which reads like a fairy tale. Prince Siddhartha Gautama was the son of a rich king of one of the provinces of India. When he was born, about 568 B.C., a *rishi* predicted a religious life for him. This so alarmed the king, who wished him to succeed to the throne, that he surrounded him with every inducement to remain at the palace. There were feasts and lavish entertainments of every description to amuse him. All evidences of sorrow and suffering were carefully kept from him. He was married to the most beautiful princess in the land, who bore him a lovely child. Yet the young prince was not happy. He yearned for a deeper truth than appeared in his pampered existence. One day, on a ride through the country, he was surprised by seeing evidences of suffering. He felt an urge to investigate the cause of this strange phenomenon and determined to escape from the palace on a search. For seven years he traveled as a poor mendicant, finally visiting some teachers and holy men for consultation. They persuaded him that it was necessary to fast in order to free the mind for deep thought. But as he slowly starved himself, he found that his thinking became less clear. He decided that this asceticism was no more helpful than the opulence of the palace had been. So he left the adherents of this method and set out alone to find the Middle Path. When he came to a spreading Bo tree, he sat down in its shade to meditate. For something like forty days and nights he remained there, seeking for the understanding that would lighten his darkness. Finally it came—the Great Enlightenment. He saw the truth, and attained the holiness and the wisdom of the Buddha, becoming the Enlightened One, the Wise. As this understanding came to him, he wished to share it with others, and returned to find his former companions in the Deer Park near Benares. Here he taught them what he had learned, and they became his disciples. His first sermon was the keynote of the new religion. We are told that "When the Blessed One began his sermon, rapture thrilled through all the universe. The devas left their heavenly abodes to listen to the sweetness of the truth; the saints that had parted from life gathered round the great teacher to receive the glad tidings; even the animals of the earth felt the bliss that rested upon the words of the Blessed One and all the creatures of the host of sentient beings, hearing the message of deliverance, received and understood it in their own language." [12]

The Buddha's teachings do not emphasize a personal God, but rather the manner of attaining holiness through moral law and of expressing it individually. It is a practical religion, not of rituals, but of a way of life. He said: "As the rays of the sun drown the darkness of the world, so he who perseveres in his search will find the truth and the truth will enlighten him. Let a man overcome anger by love, let him overcome evil with good. For hatred ceases by love, this is an old rule. The charitable man has found the path of salvation. He is like the man who plants a sapling, securing

[12] Ruth Cranston, *World Faith.*

thereby the shade, the flowers, and the fruit in future years."[13] The religion of the gentle Buddha has spread far and wide. However, in India, the land of his birth, only a small number of adherents remain today. There it has been largely superseded by the later faith of Islam.

Mohammed, the Prophet of Islam, has also a romantic life story. He was born in Mecca, Arabia, in the year 570 A.D. and was brought up by a rich uncle who was a trader. Tending the camels in the caravans which traveled up and down the land gave the boy an unusual opportunity of seeing the world and meeting all kinds of people. Also membership in the Koreish tribe gave him access to Mecca's Kaaba shrine, where he felt the impact of the primitive Arabian religion. The young Mohammed shrank from the cruelties of this organized superstition practiced by his countrymen. He felt the need of frequent withdrawals into solitude where he could think through their problems. During one of these periods of meditation in the hills, he had a vision of the Angel Gabriel, who directed him in ways of reforming the dissolute customs of his tribe. But as he attempted to put these reforms into practice, he brought down upon himself the fierce resentment of the people. They finally drove him from his home. In Medina, where he took refuge, more visions appeared to him and more plans for reform took shape in his mind. During the eight years that he remained there he was developing the details of a new religion in which monotheism was strongly emphasized. He also started to dictate his revelations, which were later assembled in the Koran, sacred

[13] Paul Carus, *The Gospel of Buddha.*

book of Islam. But a bloody battle lay between him and the general acceptance of his system. It was finally fought out and Mohammed, as ruler, moved back to Mecca, which has been the Moslem headquarters ever since. Today, in every corner of the globe, each hour of the day and night, faithful followers of Mohammed are prostrating themselves in prayer to Allah, with faces turned toward Mecca. It is to this holy center that they are commanded to make a pilgrimage at least once in a lifetime, a duty which is observed year after year.

A most touching incident in international relations was acted out a few years ago. It was in the month of August, and thousands of Moslem pilgrims had gathered at Beirut to wait for planes to carry them to Mecca. The crowd was unusually large, and the planes provided were inadequate. So the Lebanese government appealed to the United States Air Force to help transport some nine thousand stranded pilgrims who longed to reach Mecca for the Id Al Adha festival the next day. This was how thirteen of our transports became magic carpets taking off every hour with a load of grateful passengers. This was the way Christians pooled their resources with Moslems to prove that their God and our God is one.

The Moslem schools have no problem in finding the place of religion in education. Instead of being an extracurricular study, the Koran is made the basis of all subjects. Children must memorize its 114 chapters in the original Arabic. From the time they learn to talk, they are taught to repeat, "There is no God but Allah."

Out of the dim past, in Persia, emerged the figure of Zoroaster, founder of another great religion. He came bearing the traditions of ancient fire-worshipers as well as the heritage of early Hinduism. He protested the emphasis on meditation in the latter, glorying instead in industry and agriculture. The fields of the Persians were sacred to them, as well as their homes and hearths.

Zoroastrians used neither temples nor altars in their worship of Ahura-Mazda, but performed sacrifices to Him on the tops of mountains. They adored fire, light, and the sun, but only as symbols, for they declared at all points their belief in one God. Traces of this religion are to be found in the Old Testament. In a deeply symbolic sense, one might say also that this ancient system "discovered" Christianity when the Magi, probably Zoroastrian priests, "came from the east to Jerusalem, saying, Where is he that is born King of the Jews? for we have seen his star in the east, and are come to worship him." These Wise Men were students of the heavens and looked for a miraculous event to take place when the Star, probably a nova, appeared. Herod must have realized their importance when he laid plans to waylay them. But they, accustomed to visions, were "warned of God in a dream, and departed into their own country another way," to exercise a subtle influence on the future interpretation of Jesus' mission.

The sacred scriptures of Zoroastrianism are the *Avesta,* oldest books in the world with the exception of the *Vedas.* They admonish, "Keep hatred far from you. Then you will begin to replace Hate in your heart by Love." [14] In literature, both ancient and modern, and even in music, the beauties of this religion have been celebrated and its precepts repeated. Said Omar Khayyám, "Diversity of worship has divided the human race. From all their dogmas I have selected one, divine love." "The Holy One will ever be the same, the God of all." [15] "The lovers of the light are one." [15]

Unknown to these Persians and half a world away from them, yet spiritually one with them in many respects, there lived another race of "Lovers of the light." Today we know their descendants on this continent as American Indians. The most important thing in the life of the Indian is light. "Light comes before the sun, brings it forth, creates it, as it were. Hence the Light-God is not the Sun-God but his antecedent and creator. And Night is considered the mother of Day." [16] In the sacred Dawn, when Day is being born, many of the religious rites of the Indians are performed, particularly those having to do with youth, when the mind is "white," as with the clear light of day.

The absence of holy books and recorded prophets makes it necessary to approach the Indian himself in order to discover the wellspring of his religious life. His traditions have been handed down by word of mouth. Though varying somewhat in different tribes, many ceremonies are almost identical. "Certain attitudes are common to all. To the Indian every-

[14] Vergilius Ferm, *Religion in the Twentieth Century.*
[15] Jenkin Lloyd Jones, *Religions of the World.*
[16] Daniel Garrison Brinton, *American Hero Myths.*

thing about him is alive with Spirit—even sticks and stones—and he recognizes it as his task to live in this mysterious universe and get along with it." [17] His prayers are often addressed to these divine incarnations. The lesser powers are in truth attributes of the Great Spirit. The winds are the breath of Tirawa and give life to man. The sun makes things grow and is spoken of as Father, yet is not confused with the Great Father Himself, but only symbolizes fatherhood. Likewise earth is spoken of as Mother and symbolizes divine motherhood. All that Mother Earth brings forth is considered sacred. So in appealing to the heavens, the air, the earth, the Indian is addressing the lesser powers that can be seen and touched, though he hopes his prayer will be heard by the invisible One Mighty Power. Do not all religions have their "lesser powers"? Are there not many accepted interpretations of mediators between man and God? Among these, the Indian's simple nature-forms are entitled to a place of dignity.

Every stage of life has its rites, in this faith, from the baptism of a newborn babe to the singing of the Death Chant. One of the most poignant of these is the Hako as practiced by the Pawnees. It has some similarities to certain Christian celebrations. Its climax comes when its participants, led by the stars at night and the sun by day, with many a song and many a prayer, finally discover the mystic lodge they seek. Here, in his cradle, they will find the consecrated Child, symbol of all the children of his generation. He will then be anointed with living water from a running stream and blessed by the priest.

[17] Ruth Smith, ed., *The Tree of Life.*

It seems vitally important that the peaceful beauty of the native Indian's religion should be truly presented to our children at this time when so much is being done to correct past injustices to him. Also as citizenship rights are being extended to people of every race and creed, it behooves us all to understand especially the religions that are now becoming a part of the worship patterns of America. As we recognize the sacredness of each one, a measure of depth will surely be added to our own faith. And as we "learn to apply the truths of God to the actions and relationships of men," we should come nearer to achieving "a just and lasting peace among ourselves, and with all nations." So great a hope is surely worthy of the deepest consideration in all fields of education.

READING LISTS

ARNOLD, SIR EDWIN (trans.).

The Song Celestial or Bhagavad-Gita. London: Routledge & Kegan Paul, Ltd., 1948.

There are many fine translations of the ancient poem from the Mahabharata. This is one of the loveliest. The philosophical system which it describes states the Brahmanic belief held to this day.

BALLOU, ROBERT O. (ed.).

The Bible of the World. Viking, 1939.

A lay editor with the advice of two able scholars has given in this volume the scriptural essence of eight living religions. He states his reason for pursuing so difficult a project to be the desire to turn men's minds and hearts to seek knowledge of the roots of life and to identify themselves with the Power within, behind, and surrounding everything.

BROWNE, LEWIS.

This Believing World. Il. by the author. Macmillan, 1952.

This versatile Jewish Rabbi and author begins his dramatic story of religion with a picture of the streets of Jerusalem. He traces an outline of the great religions of mankind which have poured along these streets through the ages.

CARUS, PAUL.

The Gospel of Buddha, According to Old Records. LaSalle, Ill.: Open Court Publishing Co., 1915.

Derived as it is from Buddhist canon, this book has the endorsement of many prominent Buddhists. But it has special value for the non-Buddhist reader because of its excellent editing and particularly for its table of parallelisms with the Christian Bible.

CHENEY, SHELDON.

Men Who Have Walked With God. Knopf, 1948.

In this scholarly and remarkable book, the great mystics of the world from Lao-Tse to William Blake live as personalities. Their philosophies and the preoccupation of each with his own religious pattern are illuminated with sympathetic understanding. The mystic experience itself, the "walking with God," is seen to be always the same, differing only in the degree of attainment.

CRANSTON, RUTH.

World Faith—The Story of the Religions of the United Nations. Harper, 1949.

Seven great religious groups are described here and their basic philosophies outlined. The author believes that if we are to live together peaceably in One World we shall have to try to understand each other's spiritual ideals.

FERM, VIRGILIUS (ed.).

Religion in the Twentieth Century. Philosophical Library, 1948.

According to this author, if world peace is to be realized, the "various religious households must transcend their provincialism" and come together at the common level of Universal Spirit. He gives twenty-eight studies, each written by an adherent of a contemporary religion.

GREGG, RICHARD B.

The Self beyond Yourself. Lippincott, 1956.

The statement of a philosophy of life culled from many beliefs by a Harvard alumnus, a former Boston lawyer, and a onetime student of Gandhi. His experience colors his conclusions on religious faiths and universalizes them.

HUXLEY, ALDOUS.

The Perennial Philosophy. Harper, 1945.

All saints and sages, whatever their religion, make fundamentally the same report about the nature of Ultimate Reality.

KENWORTHY, LEONARD S.

World Horizons for Teachers. Teachers College–Columbia University, 1952.

This is a very helpful study for anyone teaching the children of today how to live peaceably in our present difficult world of misunderstandings.

LANDIS, BENSON Y.

World Religions. Dutton, 1957.

This book is full of statistics for those who wish to have accurate information on the chief religions of the world and the numbers of their adherents.

LEIGHTON, DOROTHEA, and KLUCKHOHN, CLYDE.

Children of the People—the Navaho Individual and His Development. Cambridge: Harvard University, 1947.

A report on an exhaustive investigation of five Western Indian tribes undertaken jointly by the University of Chicago and the U.S. Office of Indian Affairs. It is interesting particularly for its chapters on Indian children and their education. It is illustrated with photographs.

PICKTHALL, MOHAMMED MARMADUKE.

The Meaning of the Glorious Koran. New American Library, 1953.

Finding the truth and beauty of this Holy Book in a translation so accurate and congenial to critics who speak the mother-tongue should bring Western thought sympathetically closer to Moslems everywhere.

VOSS, CARL HERMANN (comp.).

The Universal God. World, 1953.

This great anthology of religious writings through the ages illuminates man's unceasing search for the ultimate reality. Here are the seers of the Infinite from many lands and centuries offering today's readers of every denomination and race renewed inspiration and hope.

Books for Young People

Elementary

CLARK, ANN NOLAN.

Little Navajo Bluebird. Il. by Paul Lantz. Viking, 1943.

Many details of Indian daily life give a feeling of intimacy with one of their children growing up in a hogan.

COATSWORTH, ELIZABETH.

The Cat Who Went to Heaven. Il. by Lynd Ward. Macmillan, 1958.

From an old Buddhist legend comes this beautiful story with its moral: The last shall be first.

JONES, JESSIE ORTON.

This Is the Way. Il. by Elizabeth Orton Jones. Viking, 1951.

A joyful procession of children of many races marches through this book together, each one having dedicated himself to the rites of his own religion. Beautiful illustrations depict the symbols of ten religions and the text consists of words from their Holy Books.

LEVIN, SALLY.

Faith and Fun. Il. by Leon Sorkin. Chicago: Goodman Brothers, 1952.

Simple verses and pictures teach the meaning of the most sacred of Jewish traditions and holidays.

MUKERJI, DHAN GOPAL.

Hari, the Jungle Lad. Il. by Morgan Stinemetz. Dutton, 1924.

To be afraid of nothing but fear is the rule of the jungle for Indian children. It is a good rule for the children of our country to learn today.

SPICER, DOROTHY G. (selected and adapted by).

Children's Prayers from Other Lands. Association Press, 1955.

These prayers are listed by countries and divided into subject groups. There are an excellent preface and occasional notes for adults.

UNITED NATIONS, written for.

A Garden We Planted Together. McGraw, 1952.

After a significant foreword by Trygve Lie, an allegory is presented of a barren field which is transformed into a flowering garden by the children of many nations.

YATES, ELIZABETH.

Rainbow Round the World: A Story of UNICEF. Il. by Betty Alden. Bobbs, 1954.

This is the story of a boy who took a trip around the world, meeting and making friends with young people his own age in all the countries benefited by the United Nations Children's Fund.

Intermediate

ANSLEY, DELIGHT.

The Good Ways. Decorations by Robert Hallock. Crowell, 1950.

With simplicity and clarity, the author shows man's perennial need for religion. She describes the various religions that have marked the world's progress and gives a brief biography of the founder of each.

ELLIS, HARRY B.

The Arabs. Il. by Leonard Everett Fisher. World, 1958.

It is important today to know the story of the Arab people, of the mighty Arab empire which so influenced the history of Europe, of the Golden Age of that empire which contributed so much to our culture, and of the Moslem religion which is so widespread now. All these things are told and pictured by two men who have lived among the Arabs and learned to know them well.

FITCH, FLORENCE MARY.

One God: The Ways We Worship Him. Il. with photographs. Lothrop, 1944.

The author here presents the three great religions of America. She describes the Jewish Way, the Catholic Way, the Protestant Way of worshiping. The book has been gratefully accepted by leaders in all these religions and endorsed by leading educators.

———.

Their Search for God: Ways of Worship in the Orient. Il. with photographs. Lothrop, 1947.

This book is an eloquent presentation of the important religions of the East—Hinduism, Confucianism, Taoism, Shintoism, and Buddhism.

———.

Allah the God of Islam: Moslem Life and Worship. Il. with photographs. Lothrop, 1950.

This book, like the previous ones, is the fruit of a lifetime of study of world religions. The liberal mind finds in them all something that can be added to one's own religion.

GAER, JOSEPH.

How the Great Religions Began. Il. by Frank W. Peers. New Amercan Library, 1954.

A book for everyone, young or old, who wants to learn about the spiritual life of humanity and the founders of man's faiths through the ages.

LIFE MAGAZINE, editors of.

The World's Great Religions, for Young People. Simon and Schuster, 1958.

Here in magnificent photography and art reproductions is a sweeping panorama of mankind's spiritual heritage.

PYNE, MABEL.

The Story of Religion. Houghton, 1954.

All the major religions and their symbols are described and illustrated here. An unusual diagram makes the living trees of religion comprehensive, both geographically and historically.

SINGH, R. L., and LOWNSBERY, ELOISE.

Gift of the Forest. Il. by Anne Vaughan. Longmans, reissued 1958.

A writer of children's books has lent her magic to a story told her by a boy straight out of India. The portrait she has drawn of a mother and her home is a model of beauty and serenity for all cultures to emulate.

SMITH, RUTH (ed.).

The Tree of Life—Selections from the Literature of the World's Religions. Drawings by Boris Artzybasheff. Viking, 1942.

Beauty and truth have been distilled from thirteen religions and brought to us in the words of their sacred writings.

Advanced

BALLOU, ROBERT O. (ed.).

The Portable World Bible. Decorated by Boris Artzybasheff. Viking, 1944.

The introductory quotation to this little book is from Max Müller: "The true religion of the future will be the fulfillment of all the religions of the past."

BENARY-ISBERT, MARGOT.

Castle on the Border. Trans. by Richard and Clara Winston. Harcourt, 1956.

Here is a story broad and deep, giving a vivid picture of a mixed group of young people in postwar Germany and describing the surge and recession of life through the seasons of the year and the seasons of man.

BOWLES, CYNTHIA.

At Home in India. Harcourt, 1956.

The teen-age daughter of the United States ambassador to India shares with us her experiences, in school and out, during her stay in India. She shows us how alike in common denominator the youth of all nations can be, and how different too, in the personal numerator.

DALY, MAUREEN.

Twelve around the World. Dodd, 1957.

As twelve teen-agers travel to a dozen different countries, they report on the young people they meet and help us to understand foreign customs.

FORMAN, HENRY, and GAMMON, ROLAND.

Truth Is One. Art director, Sayre Ross. Harper, 1954.

Reading this book and looking at its splendid photographs is an easy way of traveling around the world, learning the truths in living religions, and meeting some of the people who follow them.

GAER, JOSEPH.

Young Heroes of the Living Religions. Il. by Anne Marie Jauss. Little, Brown, 1953.

Here are the stories of twelve boys who made unique contributions to the world during their lives. Some of them lived so long ago that legend is rather mixed with history in the telling. But the truth is that each one had a vision of a faith which resulted in the establishing of a new religion.

McNICKLE, D'ARCY.

Runner in the Sun. Il. by Allan Houser. Winston, 1954.

The author of this book is a full-blooded American Indian who has had a broad education both in this country and in Europe. He re-creates the atmosphere and problems of the prehistoric cliff dwellers and makes clear the source of the Mother Corn cult. The fine pictures are done by an Apache Indian.

ROOSEVELT, ELEANOR, and FERRIS, HELEN.

Partners—the United Nations and Youth. Doubleday, 1950.

This is the first book to tell the dramatic story of the United Nations in action for and with the youth of the world. The unforgettable stories and pictures from more than thirty-five countries take on lasting meaning as symbols of the U.N. at work.

7
PRESENTING *the* BIBLE *to* CHILDREN

These words shall be in thine heart: and thou shalt teach them diligently to thy children, and shalt talk of them when thou sittest in thine house, and when thou walkest by the way. . . . And thou shalt write them upon the posts of thy house, and on thy gates.

—Deuteronomy

On account of its varied sectarian interpretations, the general opinion seems to be that the Bible best be omitted from use in the public schools. Yet, because of its great educational value, it certainly should not be eliminated altogether from the program. It is, after all, the Holy Book of our particular culture.

The Bible is the sacred book of both Christians and Jews. However, even under the hyphenated term Judeo-Christian, it is not accepted by them jointly. Many Christians overlook their debt to Jewish tradition, forgetting that the rudiments of Jesus' education and many of his sayings found their sources in the Old Testament. Jewish parents, on the other hand, too often avoid reading the New Testament to their children. Yet familiarity with this sequel to their own scriptures should be of value to them in what must rightly be called a Christian community.[1] For this reason, and many others, Bible reading in the mixed classes of public schools is highly desirable. Of course as great literature the Bible has no peer. The uncontroversial passages might well be read to the benefit of all pupils. On such occasions, moments of silence might be observed during which students would have an opportunity to pray, each in his own manner.

But Bible reading should go much further than this in a well-rounded spiritual education. I am going to speak about a deeper study of the Bible as it may be carried on in church-schools, homes, or other appropriate places. I believe our Holy Book should come very early into the lives of children, its aesthetic and spiritual aspect being given them first and later on the great stories and lessons. The feeling of rhythm lies deep in the subconscious and invites moods long before the mind is ready for meanings. Make up lullabies woven from Bible phrases and croon them to your babe. They will soothe him and at the same time sing their way into his drowsy consciousness, resting there to wake, it may be years later, into meaning and comfort.

> The Lord is my shepherd; I shall not want.
> He maketh me to lie down in green pastures:
> He leadeth me beside the still waters.

[1] The Congress of the United States opens its sessions with the Lord's Prayer.

He shall gather the lambs with his arm,
And carry them in his bosom.

He shall give his angels charge over thee,
To keep thee in all thy ways.

Yet a little sleep, a little slumber,
A little folding of the hands to sleep.

And underneath are the everlasting arms.

When a child begins to play with words, the picturesque lines of Bible poetry appeal to him. Then is the time to give him David's "He shall be as the light of the morning, when the sun riseth, even a morning without clouds." And Job's "Where is the way where light dwelleth? Hath the rain a father? Or who hath begotten the drops of dew?" And those from John's Revelation: "To him that overcometh I will give to eat of the tree of life which is in the midst of the paradise of God. And I will give him the morning star." Thoughts of such beauty water the growth of a child's soul. Perhaps that is what Moses meant when he wrote: "My doctrine shall drop as the rain, my speech shall distill as the dew, as the small rain upon the tender herb, and as the showers upon the grass."

As they grow older, children like the Bible parables and fables. For example, this one from the Book of Judges: "The trees went forth on a time to anoint a king over them; and they said to the olive tree, Reign thou over us. But the olive tree said unto them, Should I leave my fatness, wherewith by me they honour God and man, and go to be promoted over the trees? And the trees said to the fig tree, Come thou, and reign over us. But the fig tree said unto them, Should I forsake my sweetness, and my good fruit, and go to be promoted over the trees? Then said the trees unto the vine, Come thou, and reign over us. And the vine said unto them, Should I leave my wine, which cheereth God and man, and go to be promoted over the trees? Then said all the trees unto the bramble, Come thou, and reign over us. And the bramble said unto the trees, If in truth ye anoint me king over you, then come put your trust in my shadow: and if not, let fire come out of the bramble, and devour the cedars of Lebanon."

The parables of Jesus were told to people whom he compared to "children sitting in the marketplace." He used the homely circumstances of their lives to illustrate his moral lessons: "Whereunto shall I liken the kingdom of God? It is like leaven which a woman took and hid in three measures of meal, till the whole was leavened." "Again, the kingdom of heaven is like unto a merchant man, seeking goodly pearls: who, when he had found one pearl of great price, went and sold all that he had, and bought it."

The Bible is probably the world's greatest moral guidepost. The Ten Commandments were given to Moses on the sacred mountain as rules of conduct for the unsteady Israelites just released from bondage. But for us they are inspired rules for all orderly living and belong definitely to any plan of moral instruction today. Their "thou-shalt-nots" are particularly needed at this time when children seem to have been given rather too much encouragement in uncontrolled self-expression. A positive interpretation of this negative Mosaic Law, delivered from another mount generations later, is the cornerstone of Christianity. The Sermon on the Mount, preached by Jesus to the multitudes, offers a searching analysis of motives lying behind acts. The Two Great Commandments, to love God and to love man, are the crowning Judeo-Christian glory.

From the Bible we learn the meaning of prayer, most profound of all experiences on this earth. It appears to be a two-way process—man's reaching out to God, and God's fulfillment in man. It is important not to allow the validity of this experience to be relegated to the past. It must be vital to each person in his own time and in his own idiom. It was Emerson, I believe, who said, "It is the office of a true teacher to show us that God is, not was, that he speaketh, not spake." There are many Bible stories that help children to realize this immediacy of God. They easily identify themselves with the prayer experiences of little Samuel, the boy who was to become so great a prophet. Wakened from sleep by the voice of God, he cried out, "Here am I. . . . Speak, Lord, for thy servant heareth." The Lord spoke to him then, and all his life thereafter he was guided by divine counsel. In a "still, small voice," God came to Elijah out of the earthquake, wind, and fire, telling him what to do in his extremity. When the young Solomon found himself suddenly on the throne of David, ruling over a vast people, his supplication was, "Oh Lord my God, I am but a little child: I know not how to go out or come in. Give therefore thy servant an understanding heart to judge this thy so great people, that I may discern between good and bad." And because he had not asked for long life and riches, the Lord more than satisfied his request. The angel of the Lord appeared unto Moses in a flame of fire out of the midst of a bush, and the Lord called him thence to free his people from bondage. Later, in the tabernacle, "the Lord spake unto Moses face to face, as a man speaketh unto his friend." In the Garden of Gethsemane, Jesus cried out in his agony, "O my Father, if it be possible, let this cup pass from me." But then he added, "Nevertheless not as I will, but as thou wilt."

Jesus gave the only explicit directions in the Bible on the method of praying: "When thou prayest, enter into thy closet, and when thou hast shut thy door, pray to thy Father which is in secret; and thy Father which seeth in secret shall reward thee openly." Then he repeated the brief prayer devoid of "vain repetitions" which he recommended to all:

Our Father which art in heaven,
Hallowed be thy name.
Thy kingdom come.
Thy will be done in earth, as it is in heaven.
Give us this day our daily bread.
And forgive us our debts, as we forgive our debtors.
And lead us not into temptation,
But deliver us from evil:
For thine is the kingdom,
And the power,
And the glory,
For ever. Amen.

As their personal feeling for God's Word takes form, children naturally accept the spiritual authority of the Bible. Lest this come sometimes into painful conflict with certain parts of the human historical narrative, it is best to present that to them gradually. Throughout the dramatic story of the spiritual development of God's people, there appear many inscrutable episodes. Before encountering them, a young mind should be sufficiently mature to see that they have been retained in scripture not merely for human interest but as illustrations of God's purpose in the life of mankind. There are moral implications in the poetry of the Psalms, in the drama of Job, in the adventures of Jonah and the whale, of Noah and his Ark, and in many other passages that are suitable for children. The Book of Esther will give them one of the finest of all short stories. It seems to me that paraphrases and fictionized stories, though sometimes very fine, should never replace the Bible itself, which is one of the greatest books of all time. The King James Version is considered to have the most beautiful wording. Yet the Goodspeed Bible, the Moulton Bible, and particularly the Revised Standard Version, are all fine translations made by the most able scholars. The Douay Translation from the Vulgate is preferred by the Roman Catholic Church, and the Masoretic Text is used by the Jews. All these are distinguished texts. Available as they are, it is hard to understand why so many watered-down stories are popular. Children respond to the best in Bible literature as they do in most things.

In Bible teaching, therefore, an authentic text is recommended and a true historical framework. Archaeology has of late confirmed much Bible history that was formerly considered only legendary. The description of the Tower of Babel as given in Genesis has been verified even to the accuracy of dimensions and materials. The destruction of Sodom and Gomorrah is scientifically explained, as well as the pillar of salt which we are told was all that was left of Lot's wife. The wells of water "digged" in the arid south country by Abraham have been located and his tamarisk trees once more planted beside them. And the area covered by the Flood about 4000 B.C. has actually been defined.[2]

Children like to have fact sorted out from fiction, though they are quite capable of finding spiritual truth in the legends that parallel history. Both historical fact and allegory should have a place in Bible reading. The life of David offers both of these and more too. One of the best episodes in his life for story-telling is his encounter with the giant Goliath: "There went out a champion out of the camp of the Philistines, named Goliath of Gath, whose height was six cubits and a span. And he stood and cried unto the armies of Israel, Choose ye a man for you and let him come down to me. And David said to Saul, Thy servant will go and fight this Philistine. And Saul said unto David, Go, and the Lord be with thee. And he took his staff in his hand, and chose him five smooth stones out of the brook, and put them in his shepherd's bag which he had, and his sling in his hand: and he drew near to the Philistine. Then David said to the Philistine, Thou comest to me with a sword and with a shield: but I come to thee in the name of the Lord of hosts. And all this assembly shall know that the Lord saveth not with sword and spear: for the battle is the Lord's and he will give you into our hands. And David put his hand in his bag, and took

[2] Werner Keller, *The Bible as History.*

thence a stone, and slang it, and smote the Philistine in his forehead, and he fell upon his face to the earth. So David prevailed over the Philistine with a sling and with a stone, and smote the Philistine and slew him; and there was no sword in the hand of David."

Another great Bible story is that of Joseph. Set as it is in an involved plot including robbers and slaves, dreams and intrigues, palaces and jails, as well as an authentic Egyptian Pharaoh, it makes exciting reading. But more important, it contains the depiction of a sublime character. Forgiving the duplicity of his brothers who sold him into Egypt, Joseph summons them to the palace he has acquired there and saves them from famine. The scene in which he reveals himself to them is one of the most touching in all literature: "And Joseph said unto his brethren, Come near to me, I pray you. And they came near. And he said, I am Joseph, your brother, whom ye sold into Egypt. Now therefore be not grieved, nor angry with yourselves, that ye sold me hither: for God did send me before you to preserve life. So now it was not you that sent me hither, but God: and he hath made me a father to Pharaoh, and lord of all his house, and a ruler throughout all the land of Egypt."

The birth of Jesus in the city of David, his life and teachings, climax both the historical narrative and the spiritual revelation of the Bible. They also mark a turning point in world history. The ethic which Jesus preached is the ideal, however difficult of attainment, of our present society. The Great Teacher saw the divine potential in every human being. He interpreted life spiritually and taught by parable and symbol. He called himself the Good Shepherd of the sheep, the True Vine, the Way, the Truth, and the Life. "When they brought young children to him that he should touch them: he put his hands upon them, and blessed them, and said, 'Suffer the little children to come unto me, and forbid them not: for of such is the kingdom of God.' "

READING LISTS

BIBLE, THE.

All Texts and Versions.

CHASE, MARY ELLEN.

Life and Language in the Old Testament. Norton, 1955.

An enlightening study with an unusual approach. Dividing the text into three sections, the author gives a critical analysis of the ancient Hebrew mind, imagination, and language. She reminds us that history is inseparable from religion in this unique people.

CHUTE, MARCHETTE.

The Search for God. Dutton, 1949.

The conception of the Bible as the record of a search for God that was climaxed in the life of Jesus is the basis of this interesting interpretation. The author states that in it she has made her way between theological and scholarly treatises to follow the history of Israel as a sequence not of events but of ideas.

COLWELL, ERNEST CADMAN.

The Study of the Bible. University of Chicago, 1937.

The former President of the University of Chicago and Dean of the Divinity School has given us this stimulating book. It defines the tasks of historical and literary criticism and presents the material needed for orientation of a student in the study of the Bible.

DODD, C. H.

The Bible Today. Macmillan, 1947.

As this book was written from notes taken down during the author's open lectures at Cambridge University, it retains all the freshness of the spoken word. In his conclusion he answers the question: "How may a study of the Bible help toward the transfiguration of our present historical situation?"

KELLER, WERNER.

The Bible as History: A Confirmation of the Book of Books. Trans. by William Neil. Morrow, 1956.

This self-styled "nontheologian" has written a book that throws much light on Bible history through the discoveries of archaeologists. It is not to be overlooked by anyone who would like on-the-ground proof that "the Bible is right after all."

LAMSA, GEORGE M.

New Testament Origin. Ziff-Davis, 1947.

An Assyrian scholar sets forth in his book the conviction that the New Testament was originally written in Aramaic. It is an introduction to his own translation, and a provocative discussion of natural sources of the text.

SANDMEL, SAMUEL.

A Jewish Understanding of the New Testament. Hebrew Union College, 1956.

A non-technical, full-scale study of the New Testament by a brilliant Jewish scholar.

Books for Young People

Elementary

AULAIRE, INGRI and EDGAR PARIN D'.

The Lord's Prayer. Il. by the authors. Doubleday, 1934.

The tender pictures make this book a real incentive to memorizing the Christian prayer. It is given in both Catholic and Protestant texts.

COHEN, LENORE.

Bible Tales for Very Young Children. Il. by Penina Kishore. Union of American Hebrew Congregations, 1934.

In these stories the author has attempted to meet the needs of little children. Very successfully she has considered both the values of the Bible and those things that recent educational theory has taught us.

DOANE, PELAGIE.

A Small Child's Bible. Il. by the author. Oxford, 1946.

This colorful picture-book has long been the favorite introduction to children's Bible reading.

FITCH, FLORENCE MARY.

The Child Jesus. Il. by Leonard Weisgard. Lothrop, 1955.

Here is depicted a very real little boy growing up in Jewish traditions.

FORD, LAUREN.

The Little Book about God. Il. by the author. Doubleday, 1934.

For a long time this small book has been precious to many people.

GIBSON, KATHERINE.

The Tall Book of Bible Stories. Il. by Ted Chaiko. Harper, 1957.

A book filled with the wonder and the drama of the Bible.

JOHNSON, EMILIE F.

A Little Book of Prayers. Il. by Maud and Miska Petersham. Viking, 1941.

A favorite first prayer-book.

JONES, JESSIE ORTON (comp.).

Small Rain: Verses from the Bible. Il. by Elizabeth Orton Jones. Viking, 1943.

No narrative is here, but the essence of spiritual experience to be found in lines from the King James Version of the Bible.

PETERSHAM, MAUD and MISKA.

David: From the Story Told in the First Book of Samuel and the First Book of Kings. Il. by the authors. Macmillan, 1958.

Intermediate

ARMSTRONG, APRIL OURSLER.

Stories from the Life of Jesus. Il. by Jules Gotlieb. Doubleday, 1955.

A young people's life of Jesus which the author has adapted from her father's popular *The Greatest Story Ever Told.* To be had in both Protestant and Catholic editions.

BARNHART, NANCY.

The Lord Is My Shepherd. Il. by the author. Scribner, 1949.

The pictures done by this author-artist were sketched in the Holy Land. The text is reminiscent of the King James Version, which she quotes freely.

CEDER, GEORGIANA.

Joel: The Potter's Son. Il. by Helen Torrey. Abingdon, 1954.

Twelve-year-old Joel is brought into the incident of the boy Jesus's conference with the doctors in the temple at Jerusalem. The festivals and worship-customs of Jewish life are well interpreted.

KING, MARIAN.

The Coat of Many Colors. Il. by Steele Savage. Lippincott, 1950.

This story of Joseph follows the Bible record closely and much tenderness has been brought to the telling of it. Also the picture of his background and the desert life of his people is well drawn.

MENOTTI, GIAN-CARLO.

Amahl and the Night Visitors. Adapted by Frances Frost, il. by Roger Duvoisin. McGraw, 1952.

Adapted from the opera of the same name, this beautiful story tells of a visit the Wise Men paid to a crippled shepherd boy and his mother near Bethlehem. It has become a classic.

MEYER, EDITH PATTERSON.

Bible Stories for Young Readers. Il. by Howard Simon. Abingdon, 1958.

A coordinated record of human experience in seeking, understanding, and serving God is very helpful in clarifying the Bible narrative. The quotations are from the Revised Standard Version.

SCHARFSTEIN, BEN-AMI.

The Five Books of Moses: For Jewish Youth. Shilo, 1944.

A slightly abridged translation of the Torah from the Hebrew. Some important phrases are given in the original.

TRENT, ROBBIE.

What Is God Like? Il. by Josephine Haskell. Harper, 1953.

A remarkable small book of poetry that probes, with its questions and answers, the mysteries of spirit. Verses from the King James Version are incorporated in the rhythmic text.

VAN LOON, HENDRIK WILLEM.

The Story of the Bible. Il. by the author. Liveright, 1952.

No book has ever given a broader perspective to the Bible narrative than this old favorite originally published in 1923.

WERNER, ELSA JANE.

The Golden Bible. Il. by Alice and Martin Provensen. Simon and Schuster, 1953.

The New Testament. Il. by Alice and Martin Provensen. Simon and Schuster, 1953.

Presenting the Bible to Children

A sumptuous presentation of the Bible in splendid pictures. The text is given in both the Protestant and Catholic versions.

Advanced

BRUIN, PAUL.

Jesus Lived Here. Trans. by William Neil, photos by Philipp Giegel. Morrow, 1958.

Superb photographs of contemporary Palestine, accompanied by a text describing their significance in Bible history, make this an unusually valuable book.

CHASE, MARY ELLEN.

The Bible and the Common Reader. Macmillan, rev. ed. 1952.

From her courses at Smith College came this book by a great teacher who dedicated it to her students. It is a privilege for any young person to study the Bible with her through its pages.

CORNELL, GEORGE W.

They Knew Jesus. Morrow, 1957.

An introduction to the New Testament drama written from the point of view of people who lived in the time of Jesus.

GWYNNE, J. HAROLD, D.D.

Rainbow Book of Bible Stories. Il. by Steele Savage. World, 1956.

The Old and New Testaments in flowing narrative with vivid portrayals of the twelve Apostles as well as the Early Church Fathers. Fine illustrations.

HONOUR, ALAN.

Cave of Riches: The Story of the Dead Sea Scrolls. McGraw, 1956.

The exciting story of the shepherd boys who discovered, in a cave on the Dead Sea, the earliest known manuscripts of Hebrew scriptures. These have brought valuable information to all Bible students.

JONES, JESSIE ORTON.

Many Mansions. Il. by Lynd Ward. Viking, 1947.

The human narrative of the Bible is here made secondary to the scriptural unfoldment of the Word—in law, in song and story, through inspiration, and finally in the Word made Flesh—interpreted and revealed. Bible passages are in the King James Version.

KUBIE, NORA BENJAMIN.

King Solomon's Navy. Il. by the author. Harper, 1954.

The vast pageantry of Solomon's reign forms the background for this tale. It is written with authority and with a rhythm and feeling that enhance the mood.

LYNIP, RYLLIS GOSLIN.

Great Ideas of the Bible. Harper, 1954–55.

Selections from the Moffatt Bible with topics based on ancient records are interestingly arranged for modern readers.

MALVERN, GLADYS.

Saul's Daughter. Longmans, 1956.

The story of Michal, daughter of King Saul, and David the shepherd boy who came to her father's court as a musician and stayed to become king.

TERRIEN. SAMUEL.

Golden Bible Atlas. Golden Press, 1957.

This notable professor of Old Testament at Union Theological Seminary has given us a treasure in this book illustrated with relief maps and photographs in full color.

YATES, ELIZABETH.

Joseph, the King James Version of a Well-loved Tale. Il. by Nora S. Unwin. Knopf, 1947.

The skillful arrangement of this tale and the distinguished wood engravings give a worthy setting to one of the best stories in the Bible.